Collins

AQA GCSE 9-1
English Language

Target Grade 7 Workbook

Jo Heathcote and Sheila McCann

Acknowledgements

The authors and publisher are grateful to the copyright holders for permission to use quoted materials and images.

Article on pages 33–34 *The Queen's Diamond Jubilee: I have memories to treasure forever* by Gordon Rayner, The Telegraph, 5 June 2012 © Telegraph Media Group Limited 2012

All images © Shutterstock.com

Every effort has been made to trace copyright holders and obtain their permission for the use of copyright material. The authors and publisher will gladly receive information enabling them to rectify any error or omission in subsequent editions. All facts are correct at time of going to press.

Published by Collins
An imprint of HarperCollins*Publishers*
1 London Bridge Street
London SE1 9GF

HarperCollins*Publishers*
Macken House, 39/40 Mayor Street Upper,
Dublin 1, D01 C9W8, Ireland

© HarperCollins*Publishers* Limited 2023

ISBN 9780008280970

First published 2018; this edition published 2023

10 9 8 7 6 5

British Library Cataloguing in Publication Data.

A CIP record of this book is available from the British Library.

Commissioning Editor: Kelly Ferguson
Authors: Jo Heathcote and Sheila McCann
Project Editor: Charlotte Christensen
Cover Design: Sarah Duxbury
Inside Text Design and Layout: Ian Wrigley
Production: Natalia Rebow
Printed and bound by Ashford Colour Press Ltd

MIX
Paper
FSC™ C007454

Contents

Paper 1: Explorations in creative reading and writing

Paper 2: Writers' viewpoints and perspectives

How to Use this Book

This workbook contains all of the source material and exam practice questions for both Paper 1 and Paper 2 of GCSE English Language. The sources and questions have been modelled on the ones you will sit in your AQA GCSE 9–1 English Language exam. Writing space has been included to allow you to write your answers in the book.

There are a couple of ways you can use this workbook.

1. **As a set of mock exams:**
   You could set aside the correct time slot for each paper and complete the examination-style questions under timed conditions. This will help you to experience what it will be like on the day of the real exam. It's a good idea to use the workbook in this way if you are already confident with your skills.

   Once you have completed each exam, there are sample answers and AQA-style mark scheme grids for you to match your own responses against. The relevant level has been shaded in green in the marking grids.

   A good way to check your response is to ask yourself if your own answer seems…
   * stronger than the sample response
   * weaker than the sample response
   * **or** similar to the sample response.

2. **As a step-by-step skills booster and revision programme:**
   Here you might focus on one question at a time. Remind yourself of the skills you think you need for each question. Read the 'Checklist for success' to help you with this. Write your own response.

   Once you have answered a question, carefully check your response against the sample answer, making notes for yourself in the 'My checklist for success' box of any skills you might have missed. Read the 'Commentary' box, which explains how the sample answer has been structured and what effect the writing has.

   In this way you can work at your own pace and spend more time on the questions you are unsure of in order to really boost your skills.

An ebook version of this workbook can be downloaded for free. For access to the ebook, visit **www.collins.co.uk/ebooks** and follow the step-by-step instructions.

Paper 1: Explorations in creative reading and writing

Paper 1 Overview

In *Paper 1 Explorations in creative reading and writing* there are two sections: **Section A Reading** and **Section B Writing**. Questions will be based on a Source, which will be one single text.

The maximum marks for this paper are 80 marks and the time allowed is 1 hour 45 minutes. You are advised to spend about 15 minutes reading through the Source and the five questions that you need to answer before you begin writing. You should also allow enough time at the end to read through / check your answers.

In Paper 1 Section A of the exam, you will be assessed on the quality of your **reading**. You will be asked to read a piece of source material from a short story or novel from the 20th or 21st century. You are unlikely to have seen the passage before.

Your job is to apply your skills of reading and analysis to answer the questions about the passage.

You are advised to spend about **1 hour** on this section. You need to read and complete **four** questions worth **40 marks** – half of the marks for the paper.

In Paper 1 Section B of the exam, you will be assessed on the quality of your **writing**. You will be asked to write an extended writing response to either a descriptive task or a narrative task.

You are advised to spend about **45 minutes** on this section. You need to complete **one** question worth **40 marks** – half of the marks for the paper. You will be awarded up to 24 marks for content and organisation, and up to 16 marks for technical accuracy.

Section B: Writing

Section B: Writing

Responses – Section A: Reading

0 1 Read again the first part of the Source from **lines 1 to 10**.

List **four** things you learn from the extract about the narrator's neighbour. **[4 marks]**

Sample Response:

1. He had his own beach.

2. He had two motor-boats.

3. He owned a Rolls-Royce.

4. He also owned a yellow station wagon.

My checklist for success

When I answer this question I need to remember to:

- ....
- ....
- ....

Responses – Section A: Reading

0 2 | Look in detail at this section of the extract from **lines 14 to 27** of the Source.

How does the writer use language here to describe the neighbour's (Gatsby's) party?

You could include the writer's choice of:
- words and phrases
- language features and techniques
- sentence forms.

[8 marks]

Marking Grid:

AO2	
Level 4 **Detailed, perceptive analysis** 7–8 marks	Shows detailed and perceptive understanding of language: • Analyses the effects of language • Selects a judicious range of textual detail • Makes sophisticated and accurate use of subject terminology
Level 3 **Clear, relevant explanation** 5–6 marks	Shows clear understanding of language: • Explains clearly the effects of language • Selects a range of relevant detail • Makes clear and accurate use of subject terminology
Level 2 **Some understanding and comment** 3–4 marks	Shows some understanding of language: • Attempts to comment on the effect of language • Selects some appropriate textual detail • Makes some use of subject terminology
Level 1 **Simple, limited comment** 1–2 marks	Shows simple awareness of language features: • Offers simple comment on effect of language • Selects simple references or examples • Makes simple use of subject terminology, not always appropriately

Sample Response:

The writer presents Gatsby's party with phrases such as a 'corps of caterers', several hundred feet of canvas' and the metaphor of 'a Christmas tree' to describe the setting of Gatsby's party. This suggests to the reader that the parties were special celebratory occasions, filled with sparkle and light.

The impression of the party is developed through the use of listing to describe the orchestra. The repeated 'and' of 'trombones and saxophones and viols and...' makes the number of musicians seem never ending and gives the reader a sense of the scale of this massive event that happens twice a month.

The description is made more vivid through the use of adjectives such as, 'glistening' and the use of interesting verbs such as, 'bewitched' to describe the food. This creates the effect that even the buffet table is full of colour and sparkle and seems almost magical. The whole effect of the description of the party is to create the impression of a grand, glamorous event for which no expense has been spared.

Uses the text in a sophisticated way to give examples of the subject terminology.

Makes a thoughtful comment as to the effect the choices have on us.

Focuses on the detail of the feature of listing.

Gives a correct example and comments on the effect, again thoughtfully.

Shows more clear knowledge about language and makes selections of detail rather than lengthy quotations.

A more detailed comment on the impact of the adjectives and verb choice.

Makes a final overview comment, referring back to the task neatly.

Commentary

This is a very clear response that refers to several aspects of language and features. Every selection is supported with an example, but these are short and precise rather than lengthy quotations – giving one or two appropriate words. The examples and ideas are from different places in the extract, showing a strong and confident understanding. The comments on effect are all very clear, but also begin to show some original thinking and are developed in places without being too lengthy to achieve in the time.

My checklist for success

When I answer this question I need to remember to:

* _____
* _____
* _____

Responses – Section A: Reading

0 3 You now need to think about the **whole** of the Source.

This text is an extract from a novel.

How has the writer structured the text to interest you, as a reader?

You could write about:

- what the writer focuses your attention on at the beginning
- how and why the writer changes the focus as the Source develops
- any other structural features that interest you.   [8 marks]

Marking Grid:

AO2	
Level 4 **Detailed, perceptive** **analysis** 7–8 marks	Shows detailed and perceptive understanding of structural features: • Analyses the effects of structure • Selects a judicious range of examples • Makes sophisticated and accurate use of subject terminology
Level 3 **Clear, relevant** **explanation** 5–6 marks	Shows clear understanding of structural features: • Explains clearly the effects of structural features • Selects a range of relevant examples • Makes clear and accurate use of subject terminology
Level 2 **Some understanding** **and comment** 3–4 marks	Shows some understanding of structural features • Attempts to comment on the effect of structural features • Selects some appropriate examples • Makes some use of subject terminology
Level 1 **Simple, limited** **comment** 1–2 marks	Shows simple awareness of structural features: • Offers simple comment on the effect of structural features • Selects simple references or examples • Makes simple use of subject terminology, not always appropriately

Sample Response:

The text is structured through the eyes of a first person narrator, 'my neighbour', 'I watched'. This creates the effect of an observer right the way through. The narrator shares the observations with us and we witness events with him.

The text is structured around a number of time references: 'Every Friday', 'On weekends', 'Once a fortnight', 'By seven o' clock'. There seems to be an almost military precision about the parties that helps to establish the routine and organisation of them, which also tells the reader that they are regular events.

The use of tense also seems important in the extract. The narrator tells us about all of the cleaning up and preparation for the next party in past tense, 'servants ...toiled', 'oranges and lemons arrived'. The writer then switches to present tense for the event itself, 'The bar is in full swing ..... each other's names' and 'The groups change .... constantly changing light.' This allows the reader to follow the action of the party and the party-goers as though we are moving with them through the action of the event with the narrator.

Begins with a sensible choice of feature and gives two concise examples.

Makes a thoughtful and well-explained comment on the impact of that choice of narrator.

Selects a second sensible choice of structural feature.

Gives a range of examples here to prove the point.

Makes a more detailed comment here that is both sensible and thoughtful.

Identifies how tense is used to structure the text with a whole range of good support.

Concludes with an analytical and perceptive idea that is clearly explained and expressed.

Commentary

The use of subject terminology here is accurate without being over-complicated but is used well to present some sophisticated ideas.

The text is used not only as examples of the features, but has been chosen well to lead into more thoughtful comments.

As a result, this response is really quite confident in analysing the effects of the structural features of the extract, and is able to move from sensible comments to more interesting and thoughtful ideas.

My checklist for success

When I answer this question I need to remember to:

* ....
* ....
* ....

Responses – Section A: Reading

0 4 Focus your answer on this second part of the Source.

A student, having read this section of the text, said: "**F. Scott Fitzgerald creates a real sense of wealth and glamour in his description.**"

To what extent do you agree?

In your response, you could:

- consider your own impression of Gatsby's party
- evaluate how the writer creates a sense of wealth and glamour
- support your opinions with quotations from the text.   **[20 marks]**

Marking Grid:

AO4	
Level 4 **Perceptive, detailed evaluation** 16–20 marks	Shows perceptive and detailed evaluation: • Critically and in detail evaluates the effects • Shows perceptive understanding of writer's methods • Selects a judicious range of textual references • Develops a convincing and perceptive response to the focus of the task
Level 3 **Clear, relevant evaluation** 11–15 marks	Shows clear and relevant evaluation: • Clearly evaluates the effects • Shows clear understanding of writer's methods • Selects a range of relevant textual references • Makes a clear and relevant response to the focus of the task
Level 2 **Some evaluation** 6–10 marks	Shows some attempts at evaluation: • Makes some evaluative comment(s) on effect • Shows some understanding of writer's methods • Selects some appropriate textual references • Makes some response to the focus of the task
Level 1 **Simple, limited evaluation** 1–5 marks	Shows simple, limited evaluation: • Makes simple, limited evaluative comment(s) on effect(s) • Shows limited understanding of writer's methods • Selects simple, limited textual reference(s) • Makes a simple limited response to the focus of the statement

Sample Response:

I agree that Gatsby's party is presented as a perfect example of wealth and glamour. There is a sense of Gatsby trying to impress others by filling the bar with 'gins and liquors and with cordials so long forgotten... to know one from another', which suggests he may be wealthy and have a taste for the finer things in life. The writer shows us how the narrator is impressed through the use of noun phrases like 'a real brass rail' suggesting he has noticed the finer details at the party and indicating to the reader he may not be as wealthy as the host.

Everything seems on a massive scale at the party and we learn that at 'seven o' clock the orchestra has arrived,' which suggests that the host is not only wealthy but must have a huge house and garden to hold this event. The writer's use of the metaphor describing the garden as 'a Christmas tree' and the jewel-like description of the food, 'glistening' and 'spiced' and 'bewitched' creates the effect of a magical and glamorous world.

The party seems to be filled with glamorous and wealthy people who are fashionable and lively. We learn the women have their 'hair bobbed in strange new ways' and the 'air is alive with chatter and laughter'. However, nobody seems to be very genuine or really know each other as 'introductions are forgotten on the spot'. It creates the impression that people just come to the parties to be seen as glamorous and wealthy. The writer uses a number of interesting verbs to show this as the party guests 'change', 'swell', 'dissolve' and 'glide' as though there is not really anything to them. There is a 'sea-change of faces' which implies nothing is fixed or real in this glamorous world.

An original idea to open the response with an interesting choice of detail and a thoughtful original inference.

Links a method used by the writer – this time a language feature – to the point made.

Makes a thoughtful comment on the chosen feature.

Shows more understanding through another well-supported point.

A further linked method to back up the idea above, with some very well-chosen details from the text to support it.

Developing a very perceptive inference here from some well-chosen quotations.

Finishes with a strong idea about the writer's method. Does not choose complicated techniques, but uses skilful examples of several verbs to make a sophisticated point about their effect.

Commentary

This is a detailed and well-organised response. The response presents three very clear and different ideas, then uses quotations and textual details really quite subtly to support them. The level of inferential reading shows this is developing into a convincing and mature response.

The work on methods is very closely linked to the ideas and this helps to support the interpretation rather than just being bolted on.

My checklist for success

When I answer this question I need to remember to:

- ....
- ....
- ....

Responses – Section B: Writing

0 5 You are going to enter a creative writing competition.

Either:

Write a description suggested by this picture.

Or:

Write a short story about a time when a party or celebration went badly wrong.

(24 marks for content and organisation,
16 marks for technical accuracy)

[40 marks]

Marking Grid: 24 marks available for content and organisation

AO5	Content	Organisation
Upper Level 4 **Compelling,** **Convincing** 22–24 marks	• Register is convincing and compelling for audience • Assuredly matched to purpose • Extensive and ambitious vocabulary with sustained crafting of linguistic devices	• Varied and inventive use of structural features • Writing is compelling, incorporating a range of convincing and complex ideas • Fluently linked paragraphs with seamlessly integrated discourse markers
Lower Level 4 **Compelling,** **Convincing** 19–21 marks	• Register is convincing and matched to audience • Convincingly matched to purpose • Extensive vocabulary with evidence of conscious crafting of linguistic devices	• Varied and effective use of structural features • Writing is highly engaging, with a range of developed complex ideas • Consistently coherent paragraphs with integrated discourse markers
Upper Level 3 **Consistent,** **Clear** 16–18 marks	• Register is consistently matched to audience • Consistently matched to purpose • Increasingly sophisticated vocabulary chosen for effect, range of successful linguistic devices	• Effective structural features • Engaging with a range of clear, connected ideas • Coherent paragraphs; integrated discourse markers
Lower Level 3 **Consistent,** **Clear** 13–15 marks	• Register is generally matched to audience • Generally matched to purpose • Vocabulary clearly chosen for effect; appropriate linguistic devices	• Usually effective structural features • Engaging with a range of connected ideas • Usually coherent paragraphs with a range of discourse markers
Upper Level 2 **Some success** 10–12 marks	• Sustained attempt to match register to audience • Sustained attempt to match purpose • Conscious use of vocabulary; some linguistic devices	• Some structural features • Variety of linked, relevant ideas • Some use of paragraphs and discourse markers

AO4	Content	Organisation
Lower Level 2 **Some success** 7–9 marks	• Attempts to match register to audience • Attempts to match purpose • Begins to vary vocabulary; some linguistic devices	• Attempts structural features • Some linked, relevant ideas • Attempts paragraphs with some markers
Upper Level 1 **Simple,** **Limited** 4–6 marks	• Simple awareness of register/audience • Simple awareness of purpose • Simple vocabulary and linguistic devices	• Evidence of simple structural features • One or two relevant ideas; simply linked • Random paragraph structure
Lower Level 1 **Simple,** **Limited** 1–3 marks	• Occasional sense of audience • Occasional sense of purpose • Simple vocabulary	• Limited or no evidence of structural features • One or two unlinked ideas • No paragraphs

Marking Grid: 16 marks available for technical accuracy

AO6	Skills Descriptors
Level 4 13–16 marks	• Sentence demarcation is consistently accurate • Wide range of punctuation used with accuracy • Uses wide range of sentence forms for effect • Uses Standard English consistently with secure control of structures • Accurate ambitious spellings • Ambitious and extensive vocabulary
Level 3 9–12 marks	• Sentence demarcation is mostly secure and mostly accurate • Range of punctuation is used, mostly with success • Uses a variety of sentence forms for effect • Mostly uses Standard English appropriately with mostly controlled grammatical structures • Generally accurate spelling, including complex and irregular words • Increasingly sophisticated use of vocabulary
Level 2 5–8 marks	• Sentence demarcation is mostly secure and sometimes accurate • Some control of a range of punctuation • Attempts a variety of sentence forms • Some use of Standard English with some control of agreement • Some accurate spelling of more complex words • Varied use of vocabulary
Level 1 1–4 marks	• Occasional use of sentence demarcation • Some evidence of conscious punctuation • Simple range of sentence forms • Occasional use of Standard English with limited control of agreement • Accurate basic spelling • Simple use of vocabulary

Sample Response 1: Descriptive task

Misty mountains shelter the beautiful Italian house from view. They surround it. Natural bodyguards protecting this scene of loveliness and tranquility.

Cream walls hide the interior from prying eyes and it sits gracefully in the landscape. Its red roof is like a neat and fashionable hat and its towers point elegantly to the sky.

Little walls are patterned like lace and surround its gardens – all neatly clipped and green. Beautifully sculptured bushes and trees are like lush green cushions helping the elegant house look comfortable, as if it had always been there.

It casts its reflection on the lake below. The lake shimmers, calm and gentle and laps gently at the tree-covered cliffside. Sunshine peeps through the light clouds – not too hot. Just perfect.

Behind those closed doors and shuttered windows is a hive of activity. Servants sweep and clean and brush and scrub. Cooks bake and roast and grill and fry. Fashionable ladies and gentlemen dress for dinner in this beautiful house.

Outside the sounds of nature contrast with the activity inside. The gentle water, the bees in the flower gardens and a million crickets in the wilderness and mountains beyond.

Misty mountains shelter the beautiful Italian house from view. They surround it.

Annotations:

- Interesting structural feature – mirrored at the end.
- Varies the sentence structure to add effect.
- Uses vocabulary effectively and a linguistic device.
- Uses a range of punctuation accurately to present a range of ideas and detail.
- Complex spelling and more effective vocabulary.
- Using sentences for effect.
- More use of linguistic devices and details/development of ideas.
- More sophisticated vocabulary and spellings.
- Clear sense of structure and engaging ideas.

Commentary

The purpose of **describe** is consistently achieved, as is the mature register. There is a range of sophisticated vocabulary used for effect and some effective use of simile and listing. The work is paragraphed effectively and uses an interesting structural device. The work is demarcated and uses a range of punctuation accurately. Sentences are used for effect and the work is in Standard English throughout.

My checklist for success

When I answer this question I need to remember to:

- ....
- ....
- ....

Sample Response 2: Narrative task

I pushed open the gate to the house and slowly ambled up the gravel path to the front door. I could hear music blaring from deep in the house and voices ringing out from every part of the house. I knocked loudly, my knuckles reddening in the winter air. There was seemingly no response from inside and so after a prolonged pause I knocked again. Finally, the door swung open abruptly, immediately the volume seemed to double and the light, which against the murky evening was almost blinding, billowed out onto the garden. I instantly was engulfed by it all and pulled inside by a rough one-armed hug.

"Hey man, glad you could make it". I couldn't tell if he sounded tired or indifferent, probably both. Unable to think of any meaningful reply I managed to conjure up a sound of response and he immediately disappeared back into the mosh pit of teenage guests. Unable to make out any familiar faces in the jumble of conversations cluttering up the hallway, I nodded at the few who acknowledged my arrival. Squeezing between two people essentially covering the doorframe, I entered the living room. People milled around in small clusters, most of the seats left unused. A small table pushed against one wall buckled under the weight of a mountain of seemingly randomly chosen food. I scanned the room, trying to find anyone I knew. Moving to the table in the pretence of having entered with a purpose.

An hour in and having finally found some people I actually recognized from college to talk to, my evening had improved dramatically. The house was full: of people, of chatter, of music. People dancing, laughing, not a care in the world now the exams were over. Freedom.

Over the noise of the party no one heard the footsteps approaching the house or the key in the lock. In hindsight there wasn't much anyone could have done. The front door banged open, outraged yells echoed through the house and slowly from a backroom a figure sheepishly emerged. After an extended stretch of very one-sided arguing, guests slowly funnelled out, summoning parents from their beds for lifts home in the chilly midnight air. All in all, the night could have gone better.

Creates imagery through the use of interesting vocabulary.

More vocabulary and complex spellings.

Engaging use of details for effect.

Uses a minimal amount of dialogue to add to the structure and atmosphere. It becomes convincing in tone.

Varies sentences to create a sense of movement and time passing.

Uses more structural effects of listing and minor sentences.

Engaging and subtle way of bringing the plot to a conclusion.

Commentary

This narrative takes what could have been a very stereotypical teenage story and develops the idea through a strong narrative voice. The story is consistent and has a clear structure, which is added to through the use of some effective structural features. The vocabulary is interesting and sophisticated in places and helps to create some effective imagery throughout. Work is accurate and sentences have variety to add interest and impact.

My checklist for success

When I answer this question I need to remember to:

- _____

_____

Section A: Reading

Section B: Writing

In this final section of your Paper 2 mock exam, you are going to complete Section B of the paper, testing AO5 and AO6 and worth 40 marks. There will be one task to respond to.

Remember:
- *you are advised to spend 45 minutes on the exam task*
- *you must write in full sentences*
- *you are reminded of the need to plan your answer*
- *you should leave enough time to check your work at the end.*

0 5 Some people think the Royal Family are an important part of British heritage and tradition; others feel they are a costly waste of taxpayers' money.

Write a speech for a debate in your school or college about whether the Royal Family should be a part of Britain's future or whether it should be abolished.

(24 marks for content and organisation,
16 marks for technical accuracy)
[40 marks]

Checklist for success

A successful response should include:
- a clear sense of your point of view and your reasons for it
- a convincing argument, supported by well-developed ideas
- language style and rhetorical features matched to the task and audience
- a structure that is persuasive and logical.

Section B: Writing

Section B: Writing

Responses – Section A: Reading

0 1 Read again the first part of **Source A** from **lines 1 to 12**.
Choose **four** statements below that are TRUE.
- Shade the boxes of the ones that you think are true
- Choose a maximum of four statements

[4 marks]

A The Queen thanked the nation at the beginning of the weekend. ☐

B Hundreds of people gathered to see the Queen. ☐

C The Queen was celebrating her Diamond Jubilee. ☐

D The Queen did not move as she stood on the balcony. ☐

E It is rare for the Queen to speak to the nation on television. ☐

F The Queen greeted well-wishers from the balcony of Buckingham Palace. ☐

G The Queen was looking out towards the ocean. ☐

H She appeared with six members of her family. ☐

Sample Response:

C The Queen was celebrating her Diamond Jubilee.	●
E It is rare for the Queen to speak to the nation on television.	●
F The Queen greeted well-wishers from the balcony of Buckingham Palace.	●
H She appeared with six members of her family.	●

Commentary

The following statements are incorrect because:

A It mentions the 'climax' of the weekend, meaning at the end of it.

B It was actually hundreds of thousands of people.

D It says she was 'visibly moved', suggesting she was emotionally affected and that this could be seen by her actions.

G The word 'ocean' is being used metaphorically, suggesting all she can see is a vast number of Union Jack flags before her.

My checklist for success

When I answer this question I need to remember to:

- ....
- ....
- ....

Responses – Section A: Reading

0 2 You need to refer to **Source A** and **Source B** for this question:

The ways in which Queen Victoria and Queen Elizabeth II celebrated their Diamond Jubilees were similar.

Use details from **both** sources to write a summary of the similarities.   **[8 marks]**

Marking Grid:

AO1	
Level 4 **Perceptive summary** 7–8 marks	Shows clear synthesis and interpretation of both texts: • Makes perceptive inferences from both texts • Makes judicious references/use of textual detail to the focus of the question • Statements show perceptive similarities between texts
Level 3 **Clear, relevant summary** 5–6 marks	Shows clear synthesis and interpretation of both texts: • Makes clear inferences from both texts • Selects clear quotations/textual details relevant to the focus of the task • Statements show clear similarities between texts
Level 2 **Some attempts at summary** 3–4 marks	Shows some interpretation from one/both texts: • Attempts some inference(s) from one/both texts • Selects some appropriate quotations/textual detail from one/both texts • Statements show some similarities between texts
Level 1 **Simple, limited summary** 1–2 marks	Shows simple awareness from one/both texts: • Offers paraphrase rather than inference • Makes simple reference/textual details from one/both texts • Statements show simple similarities between texts

Sample Response:

On both occasions, large crowds of ordinary people come to celebrate each queen's Diamond Jubilee. Victoria refers to the crowds as 'indescribable' and for Queen Elizabeth 'hundreds of thousands of people' came to 'pay tribute'. In both cases, this would be a unique experience, and one that people would not see more than once in their lifetime. This suggests that both Queens were very popular with the general public and many people wanted to show how much they cared about and respected them.

Both Queen Elizabeth and Queen Victoria seem to be overwhelmed by the number of people present. Queen Elizabeth is described as 'visibly moved'. Similarly, Queen Victoria describes the people's enthusiasm as 'truly marvellous and deeply touching.' This implies that neither Queen expected quite such a strong response and they are both emotionally affected by this outpouring of loyalty and support. In the case of Queen Victoria this may have been because she would have had limited contact with ordinary people and would not have expected them to react with such warmth. In the case of our present monarch, she may have felt that there would be more anti-monarchy feeling and that therefore fewer people would turn up to celebrate.

Both of the Queen's use the technology of the time to communicate with their subjects. In Source A we learn that Queen Elizabeth made a rare, 'televised address' and in Source B Queen Victoria, 'touched an electric button' to send a telegraphed message 'throughout the whole Empire'. This suggests that both of the monarchs, though over a hundred years apart, were maximizing the coverage of the event through technology and sharing the experience with people who could not be there in person.

Clear statement of similarity supported by relevant quotations from both texts.

A developed and perceptive inference explained fully.

Another statement of similarity with some well-chosen supporting quotations embedded in the writing.

Perceptive inferences made about both texts.

A final clear and interesting observation with evidence from both texts.

Commentary

This response makes several very clear statements about the events, which cover a number of ideas from the sources. Each statement is supported with a good choice of textual detail or quotation and there are a number of inferences made from each text; some of which are beginning to show some deeper thought and detail.

My checklist for success

When I answer this question I need to remember to:

- _____
- _____
- _____
- _____

Responses – Section A: Reading

0 3 You now need to refer only to **Source B**, Queen Victoria's journal entry about her Jubilee celebration. **(Use lines 1 to 11.)**

How does Queen Victoria use language to convey her feelings about the Diamond Jubilee celebrations?   **[12 marks]**

Marking Grid:

AO2	
Level 4 **Detailed, perceptive analysis** 10–12 marks	Shows detailed and perceptive understanding of language: • Analyses the effects of language • Selects a judicious range of textual detail • Makes sophisticated and accurate use of subject terminology
Level 3 **Clear, relevant explanation** 7–9 marks	Shows clear understanding of language: • Explains clearly the effects of language • Selects a range of relevant detail • Makes clear and accurate use of subject terminology
Level 2 **Some understanding and comment** 4–6 marks	Shows some understanding of language: • Attempts to comment on the effect of language • Selects some appropriate textual detail • Makes some use of subject terminology, mainly appropriately
Level 1 **Simple, limited comment** 1–3 marks	Shows simple awareness of language: • Offers simple comments on the effects of language • Selects simple references or textual details • Makes simple use of subject terminology, not always appropriately

Sample Response:

Queen Victoria uses a number of very positive adjectives to describe the enthusiasm of the crowd such as, 'marvellous', 'touching' and these, combined with the adverbs 'truly' and 'deeply', really emphasise both her pleasure and perhaps her amazement at the crowd's response. We get a similar sense of disbelief and amazement in the way she starts her account using two negatives in 'never to be forgotten' and 'No one ever'. The reader gets the impression that she is both proud and delighted to be receiving such a warm and overwhelming reception.

She also uses a range of verb phrases to suggest her rather mixed feelings of both delight ('was much moved & gratified') and also concern that the whole ceremony would go without a mistake ('felt a good deal agitated'). This has the effect of presenting Queen Victoria, despite her royal status, as experiencing very ordinary and real human feelings of nervousness. It is rare that anybody goes through a grand event without worrying that something will go wrong and, even for a Queen, this would have been a unique experience.

Victoria uses the rather formal Latinate word 'ovation' to describe the cheering from the crowd, which in addition to the use of the adjective 'gratified', reminds the reader that Victoria would have been accustomed to a much greater degree of formality in the way she used language both in writing and in conversation. It adds to the impression of pomp and ceremony, which would have been a major part of this event but also contrasts to the informal way in which she refers to her own family, 'dear Alix, looking very pretty in lilac'. This creates an impression of the Queen herself and her two roles as monarch and mother because this extract is from her personal diary.

Subject terminology is used precisely and matched with appropriate, correct examples.

More evidence of terminology.

A thoughtful comment on the effect of those language choices.

Now beginning to analyse the effect of language in detail.

Using more sophisticated subject terminology.

More analysis in detail here of the effect of the choices.

Commentary

This response identifies several different uses of language. There is comment in clear detail on the effect that those choices are likely to have on a reader. These are thoughtfully developed and are showing some perceptive ideas. Throughout the answer, a range of subject terminology has been used both accurately and with some sophistication. There is a confidence in integrating well-chosen examples of all of the features identified.

My checklist for success

When I answer this question I need to remember to:

- ....
- ....
- ....
- ....

0 4 For this question, you need to refer to the **whole of Source A** together with the **whole of Source B**.

Compare how the writers have conveyed their different ideas and perspectives about the Diamond Jubilee celebrations.

In your response you could:

- compare their perspectives on the Diamond Jubilees
- compare the methods they use to present the ideas and perspectives
- support your ideas with quotations from both texts. **[16 marks]**

Marking Grid:

AO3	
Level 4 **Perceptive, detailed comparison** 13–16 marks	• Compares ideas and perspectives in a perceptive way • Analyses how writers' methods are used • Selects a range of judicious textual detail from both texts • Shows a detailed understanding of the different ideas and perspectives in both texts
Level 3 **Clear, relevant comparison** 9–12 marks	• Compares ideas and perspectives in a clear and relevant way • Explains clearly how writers' methods are used • Selects relevant detail to support comparisons from both texts • Shows a clear understanding of the different ideas and perspectives in both texts
Level 2 **Some comparison** 5–8 marks	• Attempts to compare ideas and perspectives • Makes some comment on how writers' methods are used • Selects some appropriate textual detail from one or both texts • Identifies some different ideas and perspectives
Level 1 **Simple, limited comparison** 1–4 marks	• Makes simple cross reference of ideas and perspectives • Makes simple identification of writers' methods • Makes simple references/textual details from one or both texts • Shows simple awareness of ideas and/or perspectives

Sample Response:

Although both texts are about the celebrations surrounding a Queen's Diamond Jubilee, they are very different. Source B is a diary account, written in the first person and intended to record the event, describing what happened on that day and how she felt about it. In contrast, Source A is an article written in the third person.

Throughout Source A, the writer is keen to give the impression that this is not just a celebration for the Queen's Diamond Jubilee but the event is also putting across a message about the importance of the monarchy, using the metaphor 'in safe hands' to suggest that they are an institution that will not let the country down and that they can be completely trusted. He also uses the verb 'flanked', which, with its connotations of guarding against attack, may be suggesting that the Royal Family is deliberately trying to challenge any opponents who might be anti-monarchy.

In contrast, Queen Victoria in her journal account clearly cannot imagine any such challenge and her account suggests this confidence. It is clear from the start of Source B with the use of the two negative phrases 'never to be forgotten' and 'no one ever' that Queen Victoria feels absolutely amazed at the depth of the response she has received from her subjects. This is further emphasized by the adjectival phrases she uses to describe the crowd: 'quite indescribable' 'truly marvellous and deeply touching', suggesting how overwhelmed with emotion she clearly was.

Because Source A is written in the third person, the writer cannot express the Queen's thoughts and feelings in the same way as Queen Victoria. However, the writer is clearly keen to show just how she did feel and he does this by including the Queen's own words as direct quotations, 'humbling experience', and describes her also as 'visibly moved' as she sees the crowds of people who have come to greet her. Even more powerfully, he ends his article with the words she says to the Duke of Cambridge, 'Incredible people. Bless them'. This careful selection of direct speech shows just how keen the writer is to put across a very positive picture of the Queen as somebody who cares for what the ordinary people think of her and who is genuinely appreciative that so many have turned out to celebrate this special occasion with her.

A clear comparative overview statement of the purposes of both texts.

A statement of understanding of the viewpoint in Source A.

Links this to the methods and techniques used to convey this with textual details/quotations as evidence.

A supported comparative statement about Source B that makes a clear inference about Victoria's perspective.

A further comment on methods, this time from Source B.

Another idea supported by well-chosen details.

A final inference made about the possible viewpoint in Source A.

Commentary

This response includes some key ideas that link both texts. The ideas are supported with well-chosen quotations from each text, which are concise and relevant. There is evidence of inferences having been made from both texts to show the clear understanding. There is some detailed work on the methods used in each text, again supported accurately with examples.

My checklist for success

When I answer this question I need to remember to:

- ....
- ....
- ....
- ....

| 0 | 5 | Some people think the Royal Family are an important part of British heritage and tradition; others feel they are a costly waste of taxpayers' money.

Write a speech for a debate in your school or college about whether the Royal Family should be a part of Britain's future or whether it should be abolished.

(24 marks for content and organisation,

16 marks for technical accuracy)

[40 marks]

Marking Grid: 24 marks available for content and organisation

AO5	Content	Organisation
Upper Level 4 **Compelling,** **Convincing** 22–24 marks	• Register is convincing and compelling for audience • Assuredly matched to purpose • Extensive and ambitious vocabulary with sustained crafting of linguistic devices	• Varied and inventive use of structural features • Writing is compelling, incorporating a range of convincing and complex ideas • Fluently linked paragraphs with seamlessly integrated discourse markers
Lower Level 4 **Compelling,** **Convincing** 19–21 marks	• Register is convincing and matched to audience • Convincingly matched to purpose • Extensive vocabulary with evidence of conscious crafting of linguistic devices	• Varied and effective use of structural features • Writing is highly engaging, with a range of developed complex ideas • Consistently coherent paragraphs with integrated discourse markers
Upper Level 3 **Consistent,** **Clear** 16–18 marks	• Register is consistently matched to audience • Consistently matched to purpose • Increasingly sophisticated vocabulary chosen for effect, range of successful linguistic devices	• Effective structural features • Engaging with a range of clear, connected ideas • Coherent paragraphs; integrated discourse markers
Lower Level 3 **Consistent,** **Clear** 13–15 marks	• Register is generally matched to audience • Generally matched to purpose • Vocabulary clearly chosen for effect; appropriate linguistic devices	• Usually effective structural features • Engaging with a range of connected ideas • Usually coherent paragraphs; a range of discourse markers
Upper Level 2 **Some success** 10–12 marks	• Sustained attempt to match register to audience • Sustained attempt to match purpose • Conscious use of vocabulary; some linguistic devices	• Some structural features • Variety of linked, relevant ideas • Some paragraphs and discourse markers
Lower Level 2 **Some success** 7–9 marks	• Attempts to match register to audience • Attempts to match purpose • Begins to vary vocabulary; some linguistic devices	• Attempts structural features • Some linked, relevant ideas • Attempts paragraphs with some markers

AO4	Content	Organisation
Upper Level 1 **Simple,** **Limited** 4–6 marks	• Simple awareness of register/ audience • Simple awareness of purpose • Simple vocabulary and linguistic devices	• Evidence of simple structural features • One or two relevant ideas; simply linked • Random paragraph structure
Lower Level 1 **Simple,** **Limited** 1–3 marks	• Occasional sense of audience • Occasional sense of purpose • Simple vocabulary	• Limited or no evidence of structural features • One or two unlinked ideas • No paragraphs

Marking Grid: 16 marks available for technical accuracy

AO6	Skills Descriptors
Level 4 13–16 marks	• Sentence demarcation is consistently accurate • Wide range of punctuation used with accuracy • Uses wide range of sentence forms for effect • Uses Standard English consistently with secure control of structures • Accurate ambitious spellings • Ambitious and extensive vocabulary
Level 3 9–12 marks	• Sentence demarcation is mostly secure and mostly accurate • Range of punctuation is used, mostly with success • Uses a variety of sentence forms for effect • Mostly uses Standard English appropriately with mostly controlled grammatical structures • Generally accurate spelling, including complex and irregular words • Increasingly sophisticated use of vocabulary
Level 2 5–8 marks	• Sentence demarcation is mostly secure and sometimes accurate • Some control of a range of punctuation • Attempts a variety of sentence forms • Some use of Standard English with some control of agreement • Some accurate spelling of more complex words • Varied use of vocabulary
Level 1 1–4 marks	• Occasional use of sentence demarcation • Some evidence of conscious punctuation • Simple range of sentence forms • Occasional use of Standard English with limited control of agreement • Accurate basic spelling • Simple use of vocabulary

4 One week, a station manager recorded whether trains arrived early, on time or late. The table shows the results.

	Early	On time	Late	Total
Weekdays	65	195	90	350
Weekend	30	98	46	174
Total	95	293	136	524

a) Calculate:

i) the percentage of all trains that were early .... % [1]

ii) the percentage of weekend trains that were late .... % [1]

iii) the percentage of weekday trains that were on time .... % [1]

b) In the next week, 78% of all trains were not late.

Is that an improvement on the first week? Show working to explain.

....

....

.... [2]

5 Here is some information on a packet of muesli:

Typical values per 45 g serving			
Fat	3.5 g	Carbohydrate	27.8 g	Fibre	3.4 g
Protein	5 g	Salt	0.12 g		

a) What percentage of a 45 g serving is:

i) fat? .... % [1]

ii) carbohydrate? .... % [1]

b) One 45 g serving provides 12.5% of the Recommended Daily Allowance (RDA) of protein for an 11–14 year old child.

Work out the RDA of protein, in grams, for an 11–14 year old child.

.... g [2]

c) Adults should eat no more than 6 g of salt per day.

What percentage of the maximum daily salt allowance is in one 45 g serving of this muesli?

.... % [2]

Total Marks .... / 28

5

Percentages

1 Increase each value by 20%.

a) 15 kg .... kg [1]

b) 4.5 m .... m [1]

c) 300 litres .... litres [1]

d) 0.7 km .... km [1]

(FS) **2** Decrease each value by 30%.

a) £25 £ .... [1]

b) £38 £ .... [1]

c) £299 £ .... [1]

d) £15 000 £ .... [1]

(MR) **3** Complete these percentage and decimal multiplication facts.

To work out an amount after a 10% increase   × 1.1

To work out an amount after a 10% decrease   × 0.9

a) To work out an amount after a 20% increase   × .... [1]

b) To work out an amount after a 15% decrease   × .... [1]

c) To work out an amount after a 4% increase   × .... [1]

d) To work out an amount after a .... % decrease   × 0.75 [1]

e) To work out an amount after a 2% decrease   × .... [1]

f) To work out an amount after a 35% ....   × 1.35 [1]

g) To work out an amount after a .... % ....   × 1.005 [2]

(FS) **4** Decrease each value by 22%. Round to a suitable degree of accuracy, if necessary.

a) £18 £ .... [1]

b) £512 £ .... [1]

c) 95p .... p [1]

d) £5 £ .... [1]

5 Kate buys a car for £10 500. One year later its value has fallen by 13%.

Work out the value of the car one year after she bought it.

£ .... [1]

6 A manufacturer reduces the sugar content of its soft drinks by 18%.

Complete this table:

	Old sugar content	New sugar content
Lemonade	9 g	
Tonic	11 g	
Apple drink		6.56 g

[3]

7 The population of Aytown increased by 5% in 2022.
At the end of 2022 the population of Aytown was 11 970.

Calculate the population of Aytown at the end of 2021.

.... [1]

8 Here are the prices of four laptops in a 20% off sale.

Work out their prices before the sale.

a) £319.20

£ .... [1]

b) £340

£ .... [1]

c) £440

£ .... [1]

d) £656

£ .... [1]

Total Marks .... / 29

Percentages

FS **1** The table shows the prices of some items this year compared to last year.

Item	Price in April last year	Price in April this year
Loaf of bread	£1.08	£1.15
1 litre of milk	£0.84	£1.02
12 eggs	£2.08	£2.22
1 kg of bananas	£0.79	£0.87

Calculate the percentage increase in each price, to 1 decimal place.

a) loaf of bread

.... % [1]

b) 1 litre of milk

.... % [1]

c) 12 eggs

.... % [1]

d) 1 kg of bananas

.... % [1]

PS **2** A confectionery company reduces the mass and price of one of its chocolate bars.

	Old	New
Mass	200 g	175 g
Price	£1.50	£1.35

Compare the percentege decrease in the mass and the percentage decrease in the price.

Do you think the new price is fair? Show working to explain.

....

....

....
[3]

FS **3** In a sale, the price of a TV is reduced from £399 to £260.

Work out the percentage reduction.

.... % [1]

4 An A5 leaflet is enlarged to A4.

210 mm
148 mm
A5

297 mm
210 mm
A4

What is the percentage increase in the height of the leaflet?

.... % [1]

5 The speed limit on a road is reduced from 60 mph to 40 mph.

What is the percentage reduction in the speed limit?

.... % [1]

6 Josh buys a car for £7250. He pays a 12% deposit and then pays the rest in 20 equal monthly instalments.

How much does he pay each month?

£ .... [2]

7 A sofa costs £1099. The shop offers this payment plan:

Pay 20% deposit, plus 10 monthly payments of £90

Work out the percentage increase on the price of the sofa if you buy it using the payment plan.

.... % [3]

Total Marks .... / 15

/ 28

/ 29

/ 15

Sequences, Equations and Formulae

1 Solve:

a) $4x = 20$

$x =$ .... [1]

b) $9 + x = 12$

$x =$ .... [1]

c) $\frac{x}{3} = 6$

$x =$ .... [1]

d) $x - 6 = -4$

$x =$ .... [1]

e) $5x = -15$

$x =$ .... [1]

f) $\frac{x}{4} = -2$

$x =$ .... [1]

g) $8 - n = -1$

$n =$ .... [1]

h) $6y = 21$

$y =$ .... [1]

2 Sequences of numbers are made, using a table, as shown.

A	B		C	
1	1	= 1	1	= 1
2	1 + 2	= 3	1 + 3	= 4
3	1 + 2 + 3	= 6	3 + 6	= 9
4	1 + 2 + 3 + 4	= 10		
5				

a) Complete the table. [3]

b) Describe the sequence of numbers made in each column.

A ....

B ....

C .... [3]

3 Density in g/cm³ = $\frac{\text{mass in g}}{\text{volume in cm}^3}$. Work out the missing values in the table.

Material	Density (g/cm³)	Mass (g)	Volume (cm³)
Steel		23.55	3
Mercury	13.59		12
Wood	1.5	450	

[3]

4 Rearrange the formula $s = \frac{d}{t}$ to make:

a) d the subject .... [1]

b) t the subject .... [1]

5 Complete the equations to represent each bar model.

a)

14	
x	9

$x + \text{..........} = \text{..........}$

$\text{..........} - x = 9$

$x = 14 - \text{..........}$ [3]

b)

23	
6	y

$6 + \text{..........} = \text{..........}$

$y = \text{..........} - \text{..........}$

$\text{..........} - y = 6$ [3]

c)

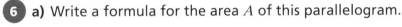

3	3	3	3	3

$\frac{x}{\text{......}} = \text{..........}$

$x = \text{..........} \times \text{..........}$ [2]

d)

32

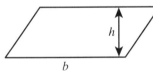

x	x	x	x

$\text{..........} x = 32$

$x = \frac{32}{\text{......}} = \text{..........}$ [2]

6 a) Write a formula for the area A of this parallelogram.

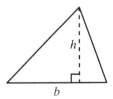

.... [1]

b) Make h the subject of your formula from part a).

.... [1]

c) Write a formula for the area A of this triangle.

.... [1]

d) Make b the subject of your formula from part c).

.... [1]

Total Marks .... / 33

Sequences, Equations and Formulae

1 Solve:

a) $2x + 5 = 17$

b) $5y - 8 = 32$

$x = $ ....

$y = $ ....

c) $4a + 15 = 25$

d) $19 - 2b = 13$

$a = $ ....

$b = $ ....

e) $7 - 3c = 16$

f) $8d + 11 = 5$

$c = $ ....

$d = $ .... [12]

2 Solve:

a) $\frac{x}{3} + 5 = 7$

b) $\frac{x}{4} - 5 = -8$

$x = $ ....

$x = $ ....

c) $\frac{m+5}{3} = 9$

d) $\frac{2x}{3} + 11 = 21$

$m = $ ....

$x = $ ....

e) $19 - \frac{3x}{4} = 7$

f) $\frac{5a-3}{2} = 16$

$x = $ ....

$a = $ .... [12]

FS **3** 1 pen costs 72p.

Write a formula for the total cost C of n pens:

a) in pence .... [1]

b) in pounds (£) .... [1]

R) **4** Luke's pay is directly proportional to the number of hours he works.

Write a formula for Luke's total pay P when he works n hours at an hourly rate of £r.

.... [1]

R) **5** The graph shows the cost of hiring a car.

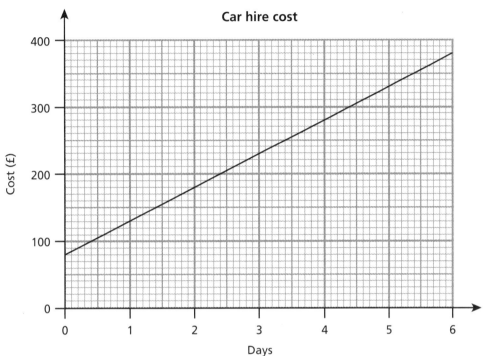

Car hire cost

Write a formula for the cost of hiring a car for d days. .... [2]

6 This formula calculates the final velocity v of an object that has initial velocity u, acceleration a and travels for time t.

$$v = u + at$$

Use the formula to calculate:

a) v, when $u = 0$ m/s, $a = 5$ m/s² and $t = 7$ s

$v =$ .... m/s [1]

b) u, when $v = 15$ m/s, $a = -2$ m/s² and $t = 4$ s

$u =$ .... m/s [1]

c) a, when $v = 20$ m/s, $u = 8$ m/s and $t = 4$ s

$a =$ .... m/s² [1]

d) t, when $v = 35.4$ m/s, $u = 3$ m/s and $a = 4.5$ m/s²

$t =$ .... s [1]

Sequences, Equations and Formulae

(PS) **7** Find the value of x in these diagrams.

a)

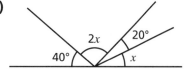

$x =$ .... ° **[2]**

b)

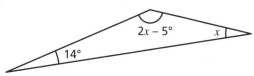

$x =$ .... ° **[2]**

8 The formula for the angle sum s of an n-sided polygon is:

$$s = 180(n - 2)$$

a) Find the angle sum of an 11-sided polygon.

.... ° **[1]**

b) A polygon has angle sum 3960°.

How many sides does the polygon have?

.... **[2]**

(PS) **9** Is 639 a term in the sequence with nth term $14n - 19$? Show working to explain.

....

....

.... **[2]**

10 **a)** Make h the subject of $A = \frac{1}{2}(a + b)h$

.... **[1]**

b) Make b the subject of $A = \frac{1}{2}(a + b)h$

.... **[1]**

11 Change the subject of each formula to the letter in brackets.

a) $y = mx + c$ [c]

b) $y = mx + c$ [m]

c) $c^2 = a^2 + b^2$ [a]

d) $x = r\sqrt{y}$ [y]

e) $A = \pi r^2$ [r]

f) $v^2 - u^2 = 2as$ [v]

g) $v^2 - u^2 = 2as$ [u]

h) $v^2 - u^2 = 2as$ [a]

[8]

Total Marks _____ / 52

1 Solve:

a) $7x = 3x + 28$

b) $5x + 7 = 2x - 5$

$x = $ _____

$x = $ _____

c) $2(x + 11) = 66$

d) $5(2x + 7) = 3x + 14$

$x = $ _____

$x = $ _____

e) $3(5x - 1) = 6(2x + 1)$

f) $7(x - 1) - 2(x - 6) = 60$

$x = $ _____

$x = $ _____ [12]

(MR) **2** Here are four equations, A, B, C and D.

A	**B**	**C**	**D**
$5x + 2 = 5x - 6$	$5x - 6 = 9x - 6$	$2x + 4 = 6x - 20$	$6x + 1 = x - 6$

a) Which equation has $x = 0$ as a solution?

.... [1]

b) Which equation has $x = 6$ as a solution?

.... [1]

c) Which equation has no solution?

.... [1]

(PS) **3** It takes 3 people 2 hours to dig a pond.

Write a formula for the time t (in hours) that it would take n people to dig an identical pond.

.... [1]

4 The formula for Body Mass Index (BMI) is:

$$\text{BMI} = \frac{\text{mass in kg}}{(\text{height in m})^2}$$

a) Tina is 1.65 m tall and weighs 60 kg.

Calculate her BMI to the nearest whole number.

.... [1]

b) Marlon weighs 76 kg and his BMI is 24.

Calculate Marlon's height.

.... m [2]

5 Rearrange the formula $\qquad s = ut + \frac{1}{2}at^2$

a) to make u the subject

.... [2]

b) to make a the subject

.... [2]

6 ABCD is a rectangle.

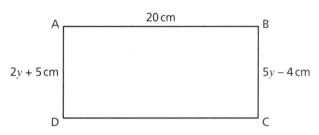

a) Work out the perimeter of ABCD.

.... cm [4]

b) Work out the area of ABCD.

.... cm² [1]

7 Line L_1 has equation $y = 3x - 4$

Line L_2 has equation $2y - 6x + 1 = 0$

Are lines L_1 and L_2 parallel? Show working to explain.

....

....

....

....

[2]

Total Marks .... / 30

Similarity, Congruence and Scaling

1 Here are some shapes.

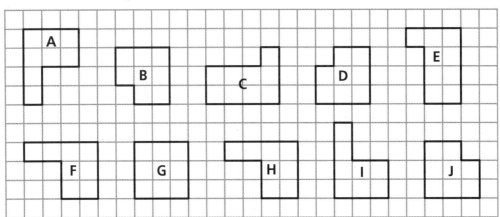

a) Which shapes are congruent to shape A? .... [2]

b) Which shapes are congruent to shape B? .... [2]

c) Draw a shape congruent to shape C.

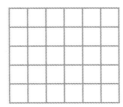

[1]

2 Triangle Q is an enlargement of triangle P.

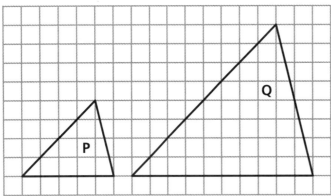

a) What is the scale factor of the enlargement? .... [1]

b) Use the correct word to complete the sentence.

           congruent   **similar**   **symmetrical**

    Triangles P and Q are .... [1]

3 Draw an enlargement of this triangle by scale factor 3.

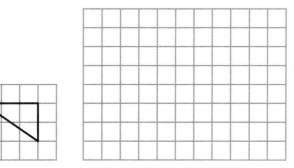

[1]

4 The diagram shows the plan of a rectangular garden. The plan is not drawn to scale.

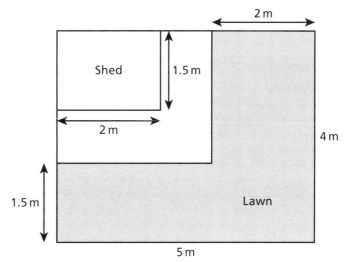

Draw a scale diagram of this garden plan on the grid below.

Use a scale of 1 cm represents 0.5 metres.

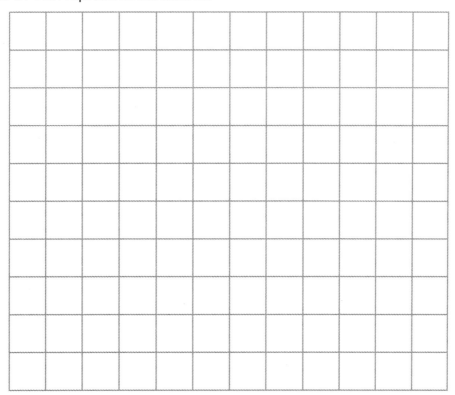

[4]

Similarity, Congruence and Scaling

5 For each shape state the order of rotational symmetry.

  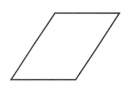

Square: ....   Rectangle: ....   Parallelogram: ....   Equilateral triangle: ....   [4]

Total Marks .... / 16

(MR) **1** Circle the two triangles that are congruent.   [1]

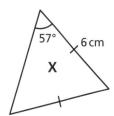 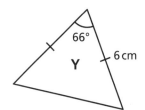 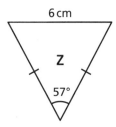

2 On this coordinate grid, shape B is an enlargement of shape A.

a) Describe the enlargement that takes shape A to shape B.

....

....

....

....   [2]

b) Describe the enlargement that takes shape B to shape A.

....

....

....

....   [2]

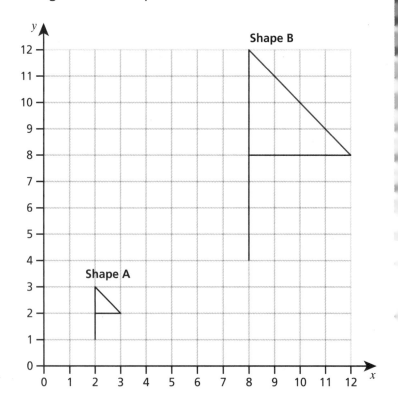

3 Rectangle PQRS is an enlargement of rectangle ABCD.

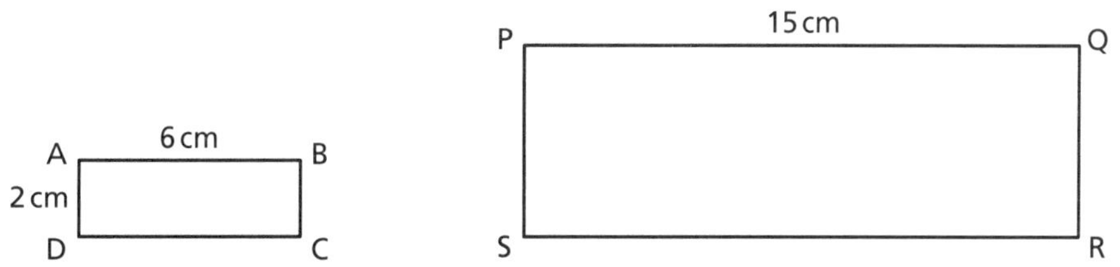

P ————— 15 cm ————— Q

A —— 6 cm —— B
2 cm
D ———————— C

S ————————————— R

a) What is the scale factor of the enlargement from ABCD to PQRS?

_____ [1]

b) What is the length of QR?

_____ cm [1]

4 Zack has a scale model of a car.

The scale is 1 cm : 50 cm

a) The real car is 4.5 m long.

How long is Zack's model?

_____ cm [2]

b) The model car is 2.8 cm tall.

How tall is the real car? Give your answer in metres.

_____ m [2]

5 The scale diagram shows the locations of points P, Q and R. In real life, PQ is 25 metres.

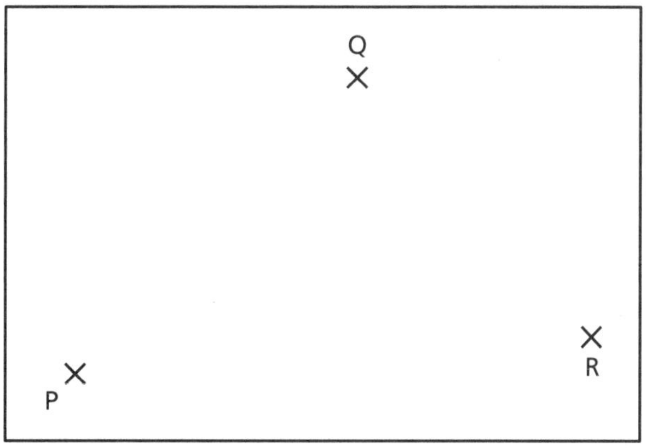

Q
×

×
R

×
P

a) What is the scale of the diagram?

_____ [1]

b) What is the real-life distance QR?

_____ m [1]

Total Marks _____ / 13

Similarity, Congruence and Scaling

1 The scale of a map is 1 : 20 000

What real-life distance does 1 cm on the map represent?
Give your answer in metres.

.... m [1]

2 The scale of a map is 1 : 25 000
On the map, two villages are 12 cm apart.

How far apart are the two villages in real life?
Give your answer in kilometres.

.... km [2]

3 Tulisa has this photograph.

25 cm

20 cm

a) She views the photograph on screen at 120%.

What are the dimensions of the photograph on screen?

.... [2]

b) She copies the photograph at 70%.

What are the dimensions of the copy?

.... [2]

4 The height of the Eiffel Tower in Paris is 330 m.
The height of a scale model of the Eiffel Tower is 5.5 cm.

What is the scale of the model? Give your answer in the form 1 : n

.... [2]

Triangles A and B are similar.

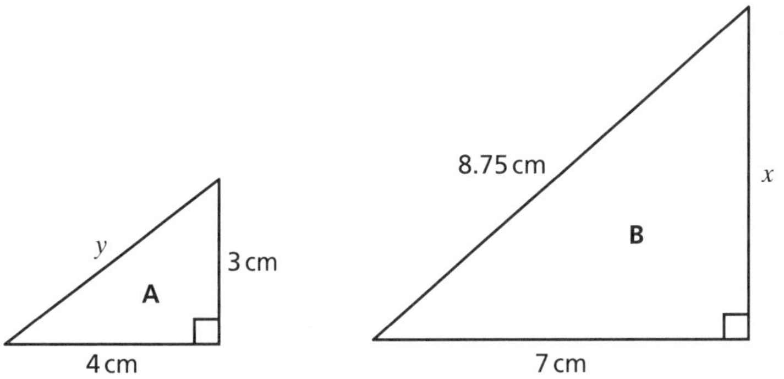

8.75 cm

B

x

y

A

3 cm

4 cm

7 cm

a) Work out length x.

_____ cm [2]

b) Work out length y.

_____ cm [2]

6 The diagram shows a white rectangle drawn on top of a grey rectangle.

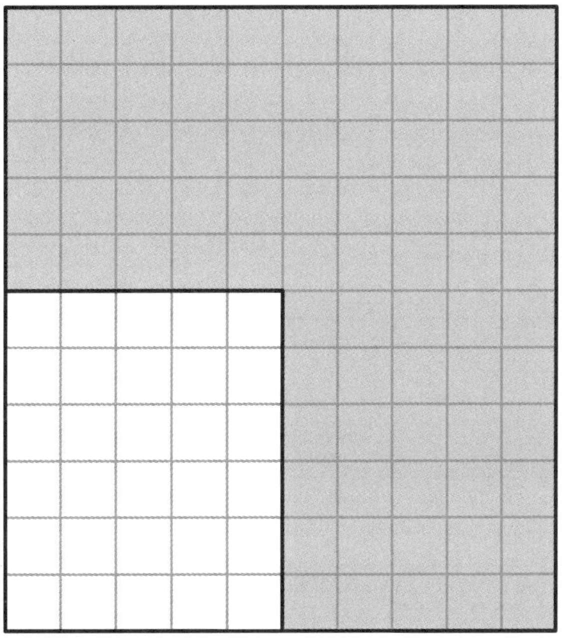

Is the grey rectangle an enlargement of the white rectangle? Explain how you know.

_____

_____

_____ [2]

Total Marks _____ / 15

	/ 16
	/ 13
	/ 15

How do you feel about these skills?
(PS) (MR) Green = Got it! Orange = Nearly there Red = Needs practice

23

Applications of Graphs

PS **1** The step graph shows the costs to hire a small car for up to 6 hours.

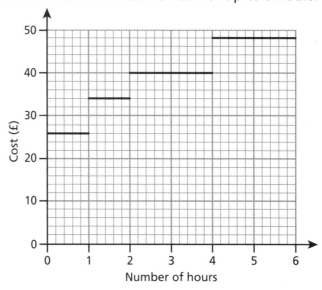

a) Complete the table to show the charges.

Number of hours, h	Cost (£)
$0 < h \leq 1$	26
$1 < h \leq 2$	
$2 < h \leq 4$	
$4 < h \leq 6$	

[3]

b) Here is a table showing the costs to hire a larger car for up to 6 hours.

Number of hours, h	Cost (£)
$0 < h \leq 2$	30
$2 < h \leq 4$	42
$4 < h \leq 6$	50

Show this information on the grid above. [2]

c) Mr and Mrs Smith want to hire a small car and a larger car starting at the same time. Mr Smith wants a car for 5 hours and Mrs Smith wants a car for 2 hours.

Who should have the small car and who should have the larger car to get the lowest total cost? Show your working.

....

....

.... [3]

2 The graph shows the costs for two taxi companies.

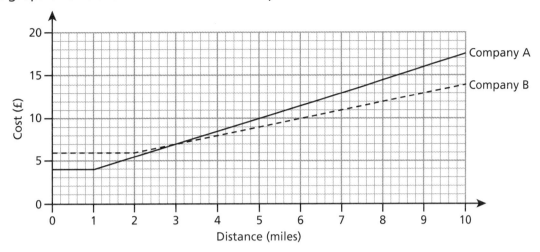

a) Use the graph to complete the table.

	Fixed cost	Price per mile (after the fixed cost)
Company A	£4 up to 1 mile	£1.50
Company B	£ _____ up to _____ miles	£ _____

[2]

b) The cost to use Company C is £5 for up to 2 miles and then £1.25 per mile.

Work out the cost using Company C for a journey of 10 miles.

£ _____ [2]

c) Show the information for Company C on the grid above. [2]

d) Jon was charged £13 for a journey of 7 miles.

Which of the three companies did he use?

_____ [1]

e) Complete the following statements.

A journey of over 10 miles is cheapest using Company _____ .

The cost with Company A and Company B is exactly the same for a journey of

_____ miles

A journey of 4 miles is cheapest with Company _____ . [3]

Total Marks _____ / 18

Applications of Graphs

1 The graph represents a train journey.

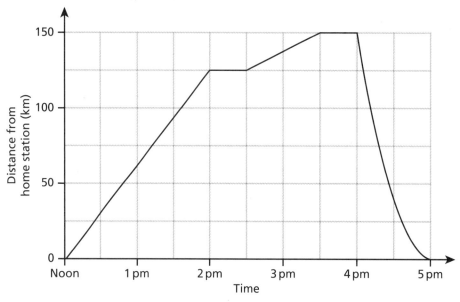

a) What happened at 2.30 pm?

_____ [1]

b) How far had the train travelled by 1 pm?

_____ km [1]

c) At what time was the train 150 km from its home station?

_____ [1]

d) Decide whether each of these statements is **true**, **false** or **impossible to tell**.

A The total distance travelled was 150 km.   _____

B The fastest speed reached was on the return journey.   _____

C The stop after the first part of the journey was 30 minutes long.   _____

D The speed on the first part of the journey was slower than the
speed after the first stop.   _____

E The speed on the return journey was constant.   _____ [5]

2 Arron, Bilal and Cain run a race. The graph shows their runs.

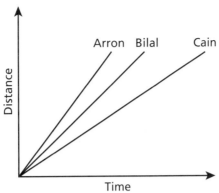

a) Who won the race? .... [1]

b) Bilal finished his race in 30 seconds.

Estimate the time that Cain finished in.

.... s [1]

3 A ball is dropped from a height of 50 metres. The graph shows the ball's height as it bounces.

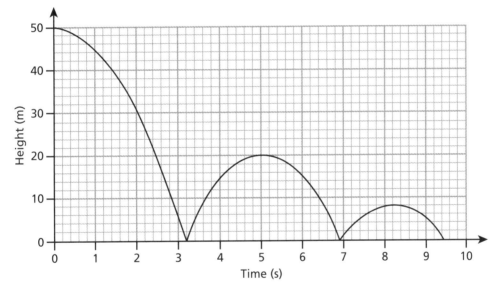

a) For how long is the ball above 30 metres?

.... s [1]

b) What fraction of its starting height does the ball reach after the first bounce?

.... [1]

c) Use your answer to part b) to estimate how high the ball will reach on the third bounce.

.... m [2]

Applications of Graphs

4 Water is poured at a steady rate into these four containers.

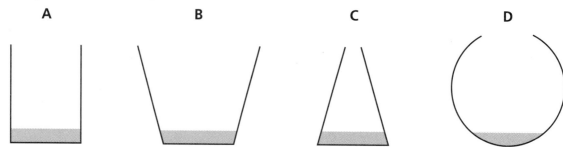

For each container, sketch a graph to show how the depth of water varies with time. [4]

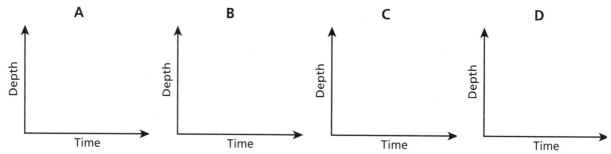

5 40 fish are put into a newly-built lake. The population of fish in the lake doubles every year.

a) Complete the table to show an estimate of the number of fish in the lake for the next four years.

Number of years	0	1	2	3	4
Number of fish	40				

[2]

b) Show the information above on the graph. [2]

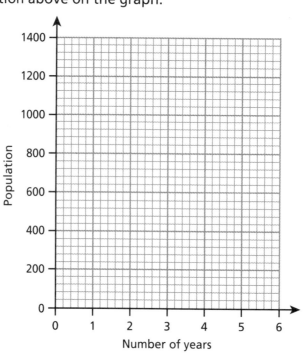

c) Use the graph to estimate the number of years it will take for the population to reach 1000.

.... [2]

1 A knock-out competition starts with 256 players. In each round, half of the players are eliminated.

a) Complete the table to show the number of players in each round.

Round	1	2	3	4	5	6
Number of players	256					

[2]

b) Plot the points on a graph. The first point has been done for you.

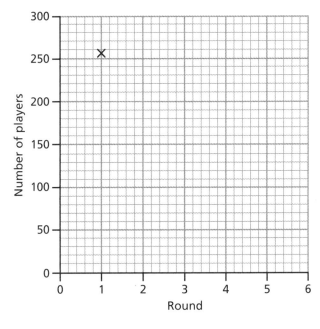

[2]

c) Explain why the points cannot be joined up with a curve.

....

.... [1]

d) How many rounds are there altogether?

.... [1]

Applications of Graphs

FS **2** £1000 is invested in a savings account paying 5% compound interest per year.

a) Use the multiplier 1.05 to complete the table to show the value of the investment over six years.

Number of years	0	1	2	3	4	5	6
Value of investment (£)	1000	1050					

[3]

b) Draw a graph to show the how the value increases over six years.

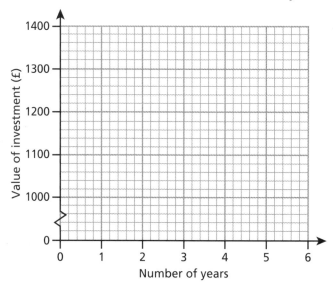

[3]

c) Decide whether each of these statements is **true**, **false** or **impossible to tell**.

A The graph is known as a linear graph. ....

B The graph is known as an exponential growth graph. ....

C Each year the amount of interest is more than the year before. ....

D Compound interest is always paid yearly. .... [4]

d) Work out how much the investment will be worth after 10 years.

£ .... [2]

Total Marks .... / 18

.... / 18

.... / 24

.... / 18

How do you feel about these skills?

 Green = Got it!
Orange = Nearly there
Red = Needs practice

Pythagoras' Theorem

1 Describe which side in a right-angled triangle is the **hypotenuse**.

.... [1]

2 Circle the letter that shows the hypotenuse in each of these triangles.

a)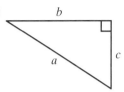

b)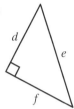

c)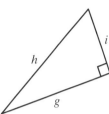

d)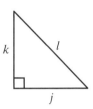

e)

f)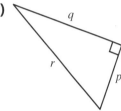

[6]

3 Jamie uses Pythagoras' Theorem to work out length x in this right-angled triangle. His working out is shown below.

$x^2 = 3^2 + 4^2$

$x^2 = 9 + 16$

$x^2 = 25$

$x = \sqrt{25} = 5\,cm$

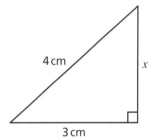

a) Explain why Jamie's answer is **not** correct.

....

.... [1]

b) Explain what mistake he has made.

....

.... [1]

c) Work out the value of x, giving your answer to 1 decimal place.

.... cm [3]

Pythagoras' Theorem

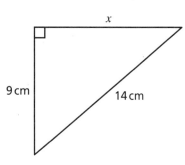

4 Find length x in these right-angled triangles. Give your answers to 1 decimal place.

a)

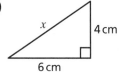

x 4 cm
6 cm

b)

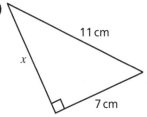

11 cm
x
7 cm

c)

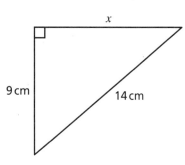

x
9 cm   14 cm

$x =$ _____ cm $x =$ _____ cm $x =$ _____ cm

d)

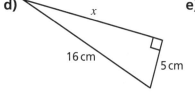

x
16 cm   5 cm

e)

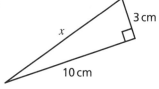

x 3 cm
10 cm

f)

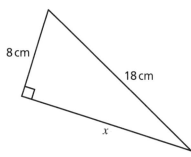

8 cm   18 cm
x

$x =$ _____ cm $x =$ _____ cm $x =$ _____ cm   [12]

Total Marks _____ / 24

1 The size of a TV is given by the length of its diagonal.

Show that this is a 60-inch TV.

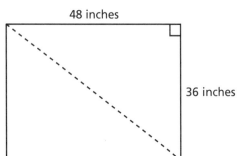

48 inches

36 inches

....
....
....
....

[2]

2 A ship sails 50 km due North and then a further 62 km due West.

How far is the ship from its starting point? Give your answer to 2 decimal places.

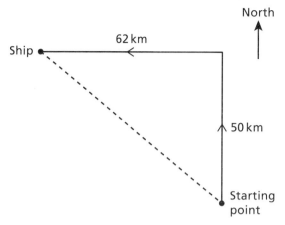

_____ km [2]

3 Mia walks 3.6 km due South from her camp and then 6.1 km due West. She then walks directly back to her camp.

Sketch Mia's journey then work out the **total distance** she has walked.
Give your answer to 1 decimal place.

_____ km [4]

4 A ladder reaches 3.7 m up a vertical wall. The bottom of the ladder is 1.9 m from the wall.

a) How long is the ladder? Give your answer to 2 decimal places.

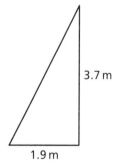

_____ m [2]

b) The bottom of the ladder remains in the same place but its length is extended by 0.64 m.

How far up the wall can the ladder now reach? Give your answer to 1 decimal place.

_____ m [3]

(MR) **5** Whole numbers a, b and c are said to form a Pythagorean triple if they satisfy the equation $a^2 + b^2 = c^2$

Work out the missing number in each of the following Pythagorean triples.

a) a, 12, 13   **b)** 30, b, 50   **c)** 20, 21, c

$a =$ .... $b =$ .... $c =$ ....   **[3]**

Total Marks .... **/ 16**

(PS) (MR) **1** Find the lengths of x and y in the diagram below.

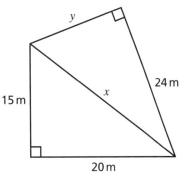

$x =$ .... m

$y =$ .... m   **[4]**

(PS) (MR) **2** Which triangle, P or Q, has the larger area and by how much?

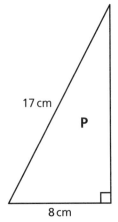

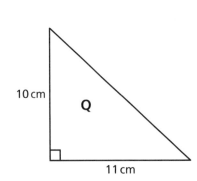

.... **[5]**

3 A triangle is shown with base 12 cm.

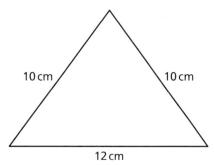

10 cm   10 cm

12 cm

a) Draw a line to show the perpendicular height of the triangle.   [1]

b) Calculate the perpendicular height of the triangle.

.... cm   [2]

c) Work out the area of the triangle.

.... cm² [2]

4 The plan of a floor is shown. The area of the floor is 84 m².
Edging strip is to be placed around the entire perimeter
of the floor.

Two-metre lengths of edging strip will be used at a cost of £5.67 each.

What will be the cost of completing this job?

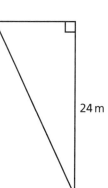

24 m

£ .... [6]

Pythagoras' Theorem

(PS) (MR) 5 O is the centre of the circle. The angle in a semi-circle is 90° as shown.

Work out the shaded area.
Give your answer to 2 decimal places.

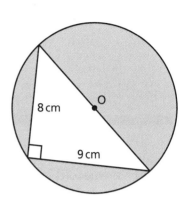

.... cm² [6]

(PS) (MR) 6 The diagram represents a square lawn. The lawn has an 18 m path running from one corner to the opposite corner.

Work out the perimeter of this lawn.
Give your answer to the nearest whole number.

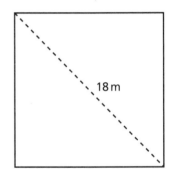

.... m [4]

(MR) (PS) 7 The coordinates of A and B are shown.

Work out the distance between A and B.
Give your answer as a square root.

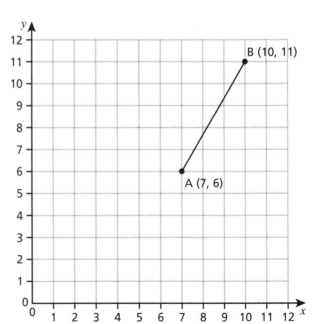

.... units [4]

8 Work out the length x, giving your answer as a square root.

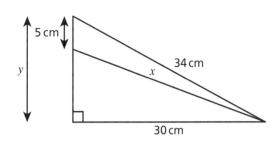

_____ cm   [5]

9 Here is a triangle with side lengths 19 cm, 24 cm and 29 cm as shown.

Is the angle marked θ a right angle? Give a reason for your answer.

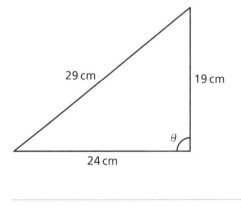

....

....

....

....

   [2]

Total Marks _____ / 41

_____ / 24

_____ / 16

_____ / 41

How do you feel about these skills?

  FS

Green = Got it!
Orange = Nearly there
Red = Needs practice

Fractions

1 Write each decimal as a fraction in its simplest form.

a) 0.7 .... [1]

b) 0.19 .... [1]

c) 0.321 .... [1]

d) 0.8 .... [1]

e) 0.85 .... [1]

f) 0.852 .... [1]

g) 0.06 .... [1]

h) 0.004 .... [1]

2 Complete this table of equivalent fractions, decimals and percentages.

Fraction	$\frac{2}{5}$			$\frac{7}{10}$			$\frac{11}{20}$
Decimal		0.125				0.625	
Percentage	40%		75%		95%		

[13]

(MR) 3 Write each time as a decimal fraction of one hour. The first one is started for you.

a) 12 minutes = $\frac{12}{60}$ = $\frac{1}{5}$ = ... hours [1]

b) 30 minutes = ... hours [1]

c) 36 minutes = ... hours [1]

d) 48 minutes = ... hours [1]

(PS) 4 Write these fractions in order, starting with the smallest:

$\frac{11}{12}$ $\qquad$ $\frac{5}{6}$ $\qquad$ $\frac{8}{15}$ $\qquad$ $\frac{2}{3}$ $\qquad$ $\frac{3}{4}$

....

[3]

Total Marks .... / 28

R **1** Write each time in hours and minutes.

    a) 1.2 hours   [1]

    b) 3.4 hours   [1]

    c) 5.75 hours   [1]

    d) 2.7 hours   [1]

2 There are 140 people on a train:

- $\frac{1}{4}$ of the people are under 16

- $\frac{4}{7}$ of the people are aged 60 or over

How many of the people are aged between 16 and 59?

                                                     [2]

3 In a flower shop:

- $\frac{1}{5}$ of the flowers are roses

- $\frac{2}{3}$ of the roses are red

What fraction of the flowers are red roses?

                                                     [1]

4 In a class:

- $\frac{5}{9}$ of the students learn French

- 12 students do not learn French

How many students are in the class?

                                                     [2]

5 Rowan and Jim share sweets in the ratio 2 : 5

    a) What fraction of the sweets does Jim have?

                                                     [1]

    b) Rowan has 8 sweets.

        How many sweets do they have in total?

                                                     [2]

(PS) **6** The table shows the after-school clubs that some Key Stage 3 students go to.

	Choir	Drama	Pottery
Year 7	22	8	10
Year 8	19	14	14
Year 9	7	17	11

a) What fraction of the students at Pottery club are from Year 9? .... [1]

b) What fraction of the Year 7 students go to Drama club? .... [1]

c) What fraction of the Key Stage 3 students go to Choir? .... [1]

d) What fraction of the students who go to Choir are in Year 8 or 9? .... [1]

e) Which club has the highest proportion of Year 8 students?
Show your working.

.... [2]

Total Marks .... / 18

1 In a bag of blue and red counters:

- $\frac{3}{7}$ of the counters are red
- $\frac{1}{6}$ of the blue counters are round
- 48 of the counters are blue
- The rest of the counters are square
- There are half as many square red counters as square blue counters.

a) Complete the frequency tree.

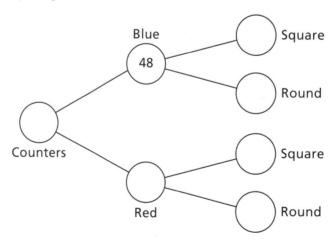

[6]

b) What fraction of the counters are round? .... [1]

2 The width of this rectangle is $\frac{3}{5}$ of its length, x.

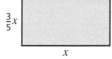

$\frac{3}{5}x$

x

a) Write an expression for the area of the rectangle. _____ [1]

b) Write an expression for the perimeter of the rectangle. _____ [1]

c) Three of the rectangles are arranged to make a larger rectangle like this:

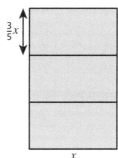

$\frac{3}{5}x$

x

Work out the perimeter of this rectangle. _____ [2]

3 Triangles ABC and PQR are similar.

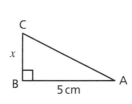 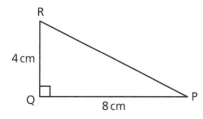

a) Write $\frac{\text{length AB}}{\text{length PQ}}$ as a fraction. _____ [1]

b) Find x.

$x =$ _____ cm [1]

c) Write $\frac{\text{area ABC}}{\text{area PQR}}$ as a fraction.

_____ [2]

4 Shay drove 154 miles at a speed of 70 mph. He then drove for $3\frac{1}{4}$ hours at 60 mph.

What was his average speed for the whole journey?

Give your answer to the nearest integer.

_____ mph [3]

Total Marks _____ / 18

_____ / 28

_____ / 18

_____ / 18

How do you feel about these skills?

(PS) (MR)

Green = Got it!
Orange = Nearly there
Red = Needs practice

Probability

1 A fair spinner has four coloured sections as shown. The arrow is spun.

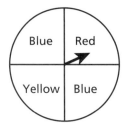

Put the letter of each statement on the scale below to show the probability of each outcome.

A The arrow landing on blue

B The arrow landing on green

C The arrow landing on blue, red or yellow

D The arrow landing on yellow

E The arrow **not** landing on yellow

0 ———————————————————————— 1

[4]

(PS) **2** These shapes are put in a bag. A shape is chosen at random.

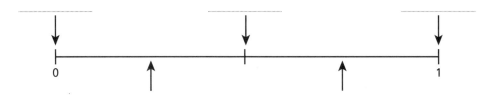

Put these statements in order of how likely they are, with the least likely first.

A The shape chosen is a triangle.

B The shape chosen does **not** have straight sides.

C The shape chosen has at least four straight sides.

D The shape chosen has exactly four lines of symmetry.

E The shape chosen has exactly two lines of symmetry.

[2]

3 Eight cards numbered 1 to 8 are put into a bag. A card is then chosen at random.

| 1 | 2 | 3 | 4 | 5 | 6 | 7 | 8 |

a) What is the probability that the card has an even number on it? .... [1]

b) What is the probability that the card has a prime number on it? .... [1]

c) What is the probability that the card has a multiple of 3 on it? .... [1]

4 A fair coin is thrown five times. It lands: Head, Head, Head, Head, Head

Jon says, "It is certain it will land on Head next time."

Explain why Jon is incorrect.

....

.... [1]

5 A fair eight-sided spinner is shown. The arrow is spun.

a) What is the probability that the arrow lands on 1? .... [1]

b) What is the probability that the arrow lands on 2? .... [1]

c) What is the probability that the arrow lands on 3? .... [1]

d) What is the probability that the arrow lands on 4? .... [1]

e) The arrow is now spun a further 80 times.

How many times do you expect the arrow to land on 1? .... [1]

6 A gardener plants 100 seeds.

74 of the seeds grow into plants.

The gardener plants another 50 seeds.

a) Use the information to estimate the probability that one of the 50 seeds grows into a plant.

.... [1]

b) In fact, 40 of the 50 seeds grow into plants.

Is this better or worse than expected?

.... [2]

Probability

MR **7** Ethan wants to know if a dice is biased. He rolls the dice 90 times. Here are the results.

Score	1	2	3	4	5	6
Frequency	19	18	15	16	12	10

a) Do you think the dice is biased? Give a reason for your answer.

_____ [1]

b) How could he improve the experiment?

_____ [1]

c) Use his results to estimate the probability of rolling a 2.

_____ [1]

d) Use his results to estimate the probability of rolling an odd number.

_____ [2]

Total Marks _____ / 23

1 Complete the table.

Outcome	Probability of outcome occurring (p)	Probability of outcome not occurring ($1 - p$)
A	$\frac{1}{2}$	
B	$\frac{1}{4}$	
C	$\frac{1}{5}$	
D	$\frac{3}{5}$	
E	0.3	
F	0.9	
G	0.41	
H	0.65	

[8]

2 A bag contains 20 balls numbered from 1 to 20. A ball is taken at random.

What is the probability that the number on the ball is:

a) an odd number? _____ [1]

b) a number less than 10? _____ [1]

c) a number less than or equal to 10? _____ [1]

d) a multiple of 4? _____ [1]

e) **not** a multiple of 4? _____ [1]

f) a prime number? _____ [1]

3 A bag contains 40 counters. Some are red and the rest are blue.

The probability of choosing a red counter at random is $\frac{1}{5}$

Work out the number of blue counters in the bag.

.... [2]

4 Two ordinary, fair six-sided dice are rolled. The total score is the sum of the individual scores.

a) Complete the sample space of the total scores.

Total score	1	2	3	4	5	6
1	2	3	4			
2	3	4				
3	4					
4						
5						
6						

[2]

b) What is the most likely total score? .... [1]

c) What is the probability that the total score is 4? .... [1]

d) What is the probability that the total score is greater than 4? .... [1]

e) What is the probability that the total score is greater than or equal to 4?

.... [1]

5 A box contains 60 different coloured beads. A bead is chosen at random and replaced. After 20 trials, 15 black beads and 5 white beads have been chosen.

a) Bel says, "This means there are only black beads and white beads in the box."

Is she correct? Give a reason for your answer.

....

.... [1]

b) Use the result of the trials to estimate the number of black beads in the box.

.... [2]

6 A money box has one of each of the following coins in it.

10p, 20p, 50p, £1, £2

Two coins are taken from the box at random.

a) List all the different amounts of money that could have been taken out.

[2]

b) Which is more likely, that more than £2 has been taken out or that less than £2 has been taken out? Explain your answer.

[2]

7 A number grid contains the numbers from 1 to 50.

1	2	3	4	5	6	7	8	9	10
11	12	13	14	15	16	17	18	19	20
21	22	23	24	25	26	27	28	29	30
31	32	33	34	35	36	37	38	39	40
41	42	43	44	45	46	47	48	49	50

Numbers are chosen at random from the grid. Here is a list of outcomes.

A: The number chosen is greater than 35

B: The number chosen is less than 15

C: The number chosen is a square number

D: The number chosen is a cube number

E: The number chosen has a 4 in it

F: The number chosen is a prime number

G: The number chosen is a factor of 50

H: The number chosen is a multiple of 7

State whether the outcomes are **mutually exclusive**. Answer **Yes** or **No**.

a) A and B ....   **b)** A and C ....   **c)** A and D ....

d) A and F ....   **e)** B and D ....   **f)** C and D ....

g) D and E ....   **h)** D and F ....   **i)** D and H ....

j) F and G ....   **k)** F and H ....   **l)** G and H .... [12]

Total Marks .... / 41

1 Ranjit puts 10 red counters and 8 blue counters in a bag. He takes out a counter at random.

a) What is the probability that the counter is blue?

.... [1]

b) Ranjit puts the counter back in the bag. He then adds another 6 counters to the bag.

He then takes out another counter at random. The probability it is blue is $\frac{1}{3}$

How many more blue counters did Ranjit put in the bag?

.... [3]

2 In a game, players roll one dice or two dice to get their score each time.

The first player to reach a total score of exactly 25 wins.

If a total score goes over 25, that player is out.

a) Josh has a total score of 24. It is his turn.

What is the probability that he wins?

.... [1]

b) Kloe has a total score of 21. It is her turn.

Show all the different ways she could win on her turn.

....

....

.... [2]

c) Ali has a total score of 19. It is his turn.

Should he roll one dice or two dice? Give a reason for your answer.

....

....

.... [3]

Probability

MR **3** A fair coin is thrown several times.

a) Complete the table to show the number of different outcomes and the list of outcomes.

Number of throws	1	2	3	4
Number of outcomes	2	4	8	
List of outcomes	Head (H) or Tail (T)	HH, HT, TH, TT		

[3]

b) Look at the pattern for the number of outcomes.

Work out the number of outcomes for 5 throws.

.... [1]

4 On one day, a café makes 30 toasties.
18 contain cheese, 14 contain tomato and
5 contain neither cheese nor tomato.

a) Complete the Venn diagram to show the
information given. [4]

b) What is the probability that a toastie chosen
at random contains both cheese and tomato?

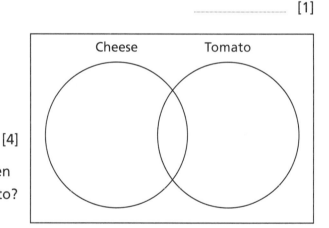

.... [1]

Total Marks .... / 19

.... / 23

.... / 41

.... / 19

How do you feel about these skills?
PS MR FS Green = Got it! Orange = Nearly there Red = Needs practice

Simplifying Expressions, Expanding Brackets and Factorising

1. Write an algebraic expression for each of these. Expand any brackets in your answer.

   a) The area of a rectangle, width x cm and length $(x + 4)$ cm

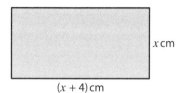

   x cm

   $(x + 4)$ cm

   .... [2]

   b) The area of a triangle with base $2x$ cm and height $(x - 7)$ cm

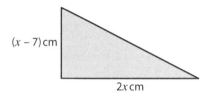

   $(x - 7)$ cm

   $2x$ cm

   .... [2]

2. Factorise:

   a) $10 + 15x$ .... [1]

   b) $28 - 21y$ .... [1]

   c) $8c + c^2$ .... [1]

   d) $6d - d^2$ .... [1]

   e) $x^2 + wx$ .... [1]

   f) $y^2 - xy$ .... [1]

   Total Marks .... / 10

1. Factorise fully:

   a) $10xy + 10xz$ .... [1]

   b) $12mn - 18mp$ .... [1]

   c) $24c + 16c^2$ .... [1]

   d) $12d - 36d^2$ .... [1]

   e) $18x^2 + 27wx$ .... [1]

   f) $6y^2 - 2xy$ .... [1]

MR **2** The area of a square is $9x^2$ cm²

Area = $9x^2$ cm²

Write down an expression for the length of one side.

.... cm [1]

3 Expand and simplify:

a) $(x + 5)(x + 8)$ .... [2]

b) $(y + 2)(y - 3)$ .... [2]

c) $(z - 4)(z + 3)$ .... [2]

d) $(w - 6)(w - 2)$ .... [2]

Total Marks .... / 15

MR **1** Draw lines to join each expansion on the left to the correct factorised form on the right. [5]

$x^2 - 16$	$(x - 4)(x - 4)$
$x^2 - 8x + 16$	$(x - 25)(x - 25)$
$x^2 - 1$	$(x - 2)(x + 8)$
$x^2 + 8x + 16$	$(x + 4)(x + 4)$
$x^2 - 50x + 625$	$(x - 1)(x + 1)$
$x^2 + 6x - 16$	$(x - 5)(x + 5)$
$x^2 - 25$	$(x - 4)(x + 4)$

2 Write an expression for the area of this square. Expand and simplify your answer.

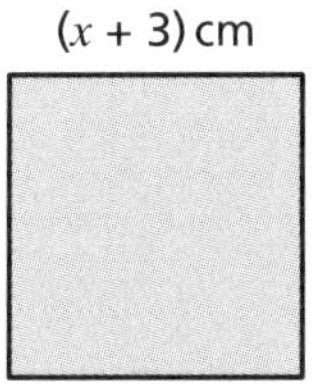

(x + 3) cm

.... [2]

3 The small white rectangle is cut out of the large rectangle.

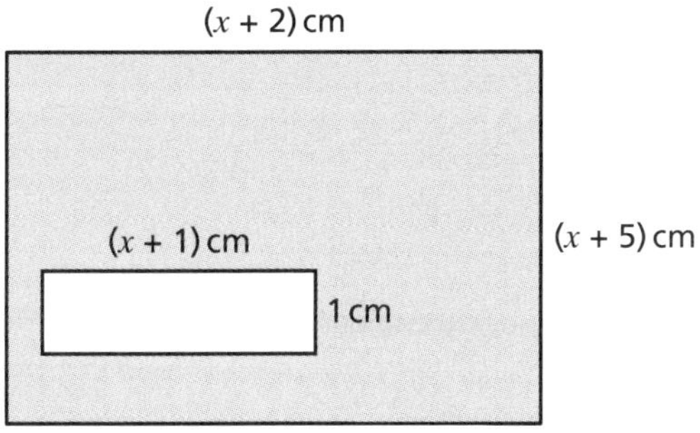

(x + 2) cm
(x + 5) cm
(x + 1) cm
1 cm

Write and simplify an expression for the shaded area. .... [2]

4 Expand and simplify $(x + 2)(x + 3)(x - 4)$

.... [3]

5 The diagram shows a cuboid.

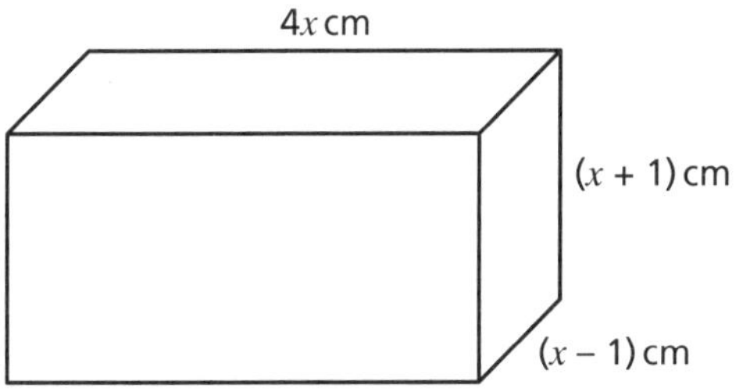

4x cm
(x + 1) cm
(x – 1) cm

a) Show that an expression for the volume of the cuboid is $4x^3 - 4x$

....

.... [2]

b) Show that when $x = 2$, the volume of the cuboid is $24\,\text{cm}^3$

....

.... [2]

Total Marks .... / 16

.... / 10

.... / 15

.... / 16

How do you feel about these skills?

PS MR

Green = Got it!

Orange = Nearly there

Red = Needs practice

Standard Form

1. Write each power of 10 as a decimal number.

   Example: $10^3 = 1000$

   a) $10^6 =$ _____   b) $10^5 =$ _____   c) $10^2 =$ _____   [3]

2. Write each power of 10 as a fraction and a decimal.

   a) $10^{-2} = \frac{1}{100} =$ _____   b) $10^{-4} = \frac{1}{\boxed{}} =$ 0.0001

   c) $10^{-1} = \frac{1}{\boxed{}} =$ _____   d) $10^{-3} = \frac{1}{\boxed{}} =$ _____   [6]

3. Complete these multiplications.

   a) $10^2 \times 10^3 = 10^{\boxed{}}$ b) $10^{-2} \times 10^3 = 10^{\boxed{}} =$ _____

   c) $10^{-1} \times 10^{-2} = 10^{\boxed{}}$ d) $10^{-3} \times 10^3 = 10^{\boxed{}} =$ _____   [6]

4. Complete these divisions.

   a) $10^5 \div 10^3 = 10^{\boxed{}}$ b) $10^4 \div 10^2 = 10^{\boxed{}}$

   c) $10^1 \div 10^3 = 10^{\boxed{}}$ d) $10^4 \div 10^4 = 10^{\boxed{}} =$ _____   [5]

(MR) 5. Complete these calculations to make each one equal to 42.

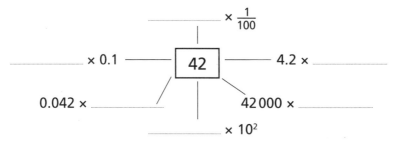

_____ $\times \frac{1}{100}$

_____ $\times 0.1$ —— 42 —— $4.2 \times$ _____

$0.042 \times$ _____ $42\,000 \times$ _____

_____ $\times 10^2$ [6]

6. Draw lines to match each prefix to a power of 10.

giga		10^{-3}
nano		10^6
mega		10^3
milli		10^9
kilo		10^{-6}
micro		10^{-9}

   [4]

Total Marks _____ / 30

1 Write each number as an ordinary number.

a) 8.1×10^3 .... [1]

b) 4.5×10^5 .... [1]

c) 1.2×10^6 .... [1]

d) 5.06×10^2 .... [1]

e) 7.9×10^8 .... [1]

f) 3.15×10^4 .... [1]

2 Write each number in standard form.

a) 5200 .... [1]

b) 350 .... [1]

c) 4070 .... [1]

d) 125 000 .... [1]

e) 27 .... [1]

f) 2 005 000 .... [1]

3 a) 37×10^4 is **not** in standard form.

Explain why.

....

.... [1]

b) Complete the working to write 37×10^4 in standard form.

$37 \times 10^4 = 3.7 \times \underline{\hspace{2cm}} \times 10^4$

$= 3.7 \times 10^{\square}$ [2]

4 Write these numbers in standard form.

a) 26×10^3 .... [1]

b) 510×10^4 .... [1]

c) 307×10^2 .... [1]

d) 33.2×10^4 .... [1]

Standard Form

(MR) **5** **a)** 0.26×10^3 is **not** in standard form.

Explain why.

_____ [1]

b) Complete the working to write 0.26×10^3 in standard form.

$0.26 \times 10^3 = 2.6 \times \dfrac{1}{\boxed{}} \times 10^3$

$ = 2.6 \times 10^{\boxed{}} \times 10^3$

$ = 2.6 \times 10^{\boxed{}}$ [3]

(PS) **6** Write these numbers in order, starting with the smallest.

4.5×10^5 $\qquad$ 3.7×10^5 $\qquad$ 8.2×10^3 $\qquad$ 1.6×10^6 $\qquad$ 3.7×10^3

_____ [3]

7 Mandeep's phone has 32 GB (gigabytes) of storage. 1 GB = 1 000 000 000 bytes

Write 32 GB in standard form.

_____ [2]

(PS) **8** 1 MB (megabyte) = 10^6 bytes

How many times bigger is a gigabyte than a megabyte?

_____ [1]

Total Marks _____ / 29

1 Write each number as a decimal number.

a) 2×10^{-2} _____ [1]

b) 3.5×10^{-5} _____ [1]

c) 1.6×10^{-1} _____ [1]

d) 7.2×10^{-4} _____ [1]

e) 5.07×10^{-6} _____ [1]

f) 4×10^{-5} _____ [1]

2 Write each number in standard form.

a) 0.005 _____ [1]

b) 0.604 _____ [1]

c) 0.00025 _____ [1]

d) 0.0000516 _____ [1]

e) 0.003 _____ [1]

f) 0.0000071 _____ [1]

3 Complete the working to write 0.052×10^{-5} in standard form.

$$0.052 \times 10^{-5} = 5.2 \times \text{\underline{\hspace{2cm}}} \times 10^{-5}$$

$$= 5.2 \times 10^{\boxed{}}$$ [2]

4 By considering the size of each measurement, match each option in the box to its distance below.

| 2.75×10^{-10} metres | 2.095×10^{11} metres | 1.7×10^{7} metres |

a) The distance from London to Sydney, Australia _____ [1]

b) The distance from Earth to Mars _____ [1]

c) The diameter of a water molecule _____ [1]

5 The table shows some information about the planets of the Solar System.

Planet	Distance from Sun (km)	Diameter (km)
Earth	1.496×10^{8}	1.2756×10^{4}
Jupiter	7.783×10^{8}	1.42796×10^{5}
Mars	2.279×10^{8}	6.787×10^{3}
Mercury	5.79×10^{7}	4.878×10^{3}
Neptune	4.4971×10^{9}	4.86×10^{4}
Saturn	1.427×10^{9}	1.2066×10^{5}
Uranus	2.871×10^{9}	5.1118×10^{4}
Venus	1.082×10^{8}	1.2104×10^{4}

Which planet:

a) is closest to the Sun? _____ [1]

b) is furthest from the Sun? _____ [1]

c) has the greatest diameter? _____ [1]

d) has the smallest diameter? _____ [1]

e) has a diameter approximately 10 times greater than Mercury? _____ [1]

6 There are 3.35×10^{25} water molecules in 1 litre of water.

Calculate the number of water molecules in the following.
Give your answers in standard form.

a) 2 litres of water

.... [1]

b) 5 litres of water

.... [2]

7 A hayfever tablet weighs 1×10^{-3} grams.

Work out the mass of 120 of these hayfever tablets.
Write your answer in standard form.

.... g [1]

8 In 2020, the Earth's population was estimated to be 7.753 billion.

1 billion is 1000 million.

a) Write the Earth's 2020 population in standard form.

.... [1]

b) In 1920, the Earth's population was estimated to be 1.7 billion.

Use a calculator to work out how many times greater the 2020 population was than the 1920 population.

.... [2]

Total Marks .... / 29

.... / 30

.... / 29

.... / 29

How do you feel about these skills?
PS   MR   Green = Got it! Orange = Nearly there Red = Needs practice

2 **a)** A driver puts 68 litres of fuel in his car. It takes 2 minutes.

What is the rate of flow? .... litres/minute [1]

b) Another driver uses the same pump and takes 30 seconds to fill his tank. The fuel costs £1.90 per litre.

Work out the amount paid and state the assumption you made.

£ ....

Assumption: .... [3]

3 A vegan sauce comes in two sizes:

- 100 grams costs £2.40

- 250 grams costs £6.19

Work out the cost per gram for each size and decide which is the better value.

.... [2]

4 Gluten-free pasta costs £0.85 for 500 grams or £0.72 for 400 grams.

Work out the cost per 100 grams for each and decide which is the better value.

.... [2]

Total Marks .... / 13

1 A 550 g pack of cheese costs £4.00. A 350 g pack costs £3.80. A 180 g grated pack costs £1.50

Sort the three packs into order of value for money, starting with the best value.

.... g pack, ... g pack, ... g pack [3]

2 **a)** Show that 5 m/s is the same as 18 km/h.

.... [2]

b) Convert 12.5 m/s into km/h.

.... km/h [2]

FS **PS** **3** Sofia and Manuel are waiters. They both earn exactly the same amount of pay each week.

Sofia works for 30 hours and is paid £15.36 per hour. Manuel works for 36 hours each week.

a) Work out how much Manuel is paid per hour.

£ .... [2]

b) Work out how much more Sofia would earn per week if she increased her working hours to the same as Manuel.

£ .... [2]

FS **PS** **4** **Density = $\frac{mass}{volume}$**

The density of gold is 19.3 g/cm³
The value of the gold is £52 per gram.
The diagram shows a block of gold in the shape
of a cuboid.

12 cm

3 cm

2 cm

a) Work out the value of the block.

£ .... [3]

b) The block of gold is used to make rings. Each ring uses 3 grams of gold.
The average price each ring is sold for is £250.

Work out the profit if all the rings are sold. Ignore any other costs.

£ .... [3]

Total Marks .... / 17

.... / 17

.... / 13

.... / 17

How do you feel about these skills?
PS **MR** **FS**   Green = Got it! Orange = Nearly there Red = Needs practice

Right-angled Triangles

1 Use your calculator to find each value. Round values to 4 decimal places if necessary.

a) sin 30° ....   **b)** tan 45° ....

c) cos 40° ....   **d)** sin 82° .... [4]

2 Complete the trigonometric ratios for this triangle:

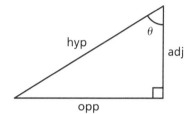

a) $\cos \theta = \dfrac{}{\text{hyp}}$ **b)** $\sin \theta = \dfrac{}{}$ **c)** $\tan \theta = \dfrac{}{}$ [3]

3 Complete the working to find the length of each side labelled with a letter.
Give your answers to 1 decimal place.

a)

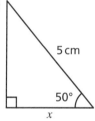

$\cos 50° = \dfrac{x}{\rule{1cm}{0.4pt}}$

$\rule{1.5cm}{0.4pt} \times \cos 50° = x$

$x = \rule{1.5cm}{0.4pt}$ cm (1 d.p.)   [3]

b)

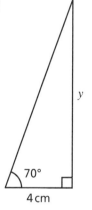

$\tan 70° = \dfrac{\rule{1cm}{0.4pt}}{\rule{1cm}{0.4pt}}$

$\rule{1.5cm}{0.4pt} \times \tan 70° = y$

$y = \rule{1.5cm}{0.4pt}$ cm (1 d.p.)   [3]

c)

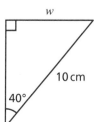

$\rule{1.5cm}{0.4pt}\, 40° = \dfrac{w}{\rule{1cm}{0.4pt}}$

$10 \rule{1.5cm}{0.4pt}\, 40° = w$

$w = \rule{1.5cm}{0.4pt}$ cm (1 d.p.)   [3]

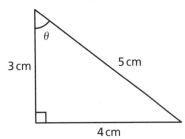

Right-angled Triangles

4 For this triangle, write the ratios as fractions.

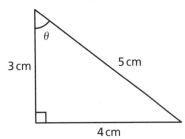

a) sin θ = ...

b) tan θ = ...

c) cos θ = ... **[3]**

5 Find the length of each side labelled with a letter. Give your answers to 1 decimal place.

a)

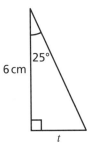

t = ... cm **[3]**

b)

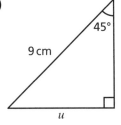

u = ... cm **[3]**

c)

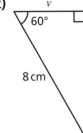

v = ... cm **[3]**

d)

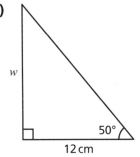

w = ... cm **[3]**

Total Marks .... / 31

1 Solve to find the value of each letter. Give your answers to 1 decimal place if necessary. The first one has been started for you.

a) sin m = 0.842

m = sin^{-1}(0.842) = ...

b) tan n = 2.4

n = ...

c) cos p = $\frac{\sqrt{3}}{2}$

p = ...

d) sin q = $\frac{1}{\sqrt{2}}$

q = ... **[4]**

2 Complete the working to find the size of angle θ in each diagram.
Give your answers to 1 decimal place.

a)

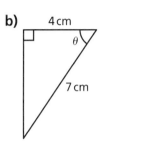

$\tan \theta = \dfrac{\rule{1cm}{0.4pt}}{\rule{1cm}{0.4pt}}$

$\theta = \tan^{-1}\left(\dfrac{\rule{0.8cm}{0.4pt}}{\rule{0.8cm}{0.4pt}}\right)$

$\theta = $ .... (1 d.p.)   [3]

b)

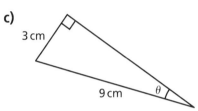

.... $\theta = \dfrac{4}{7}$

$\theta = $ .... $\left(\dfrac{4}{7}\right)$

$\theta = $ .... (1 d.p.)   [3]

c)

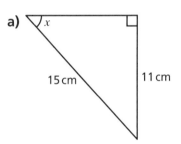

.... $\theta = \dfrac{3}{9}$

$\theta = $ .... $\left(\dfrac{3}{9}\right)$

$\theta = $ .... (1 d.p.)   [3]

3 Find the size of each lettered angle. Give your answers to 1 decimal place.

a)

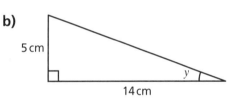

$x = $ .... °   [3]

b)

$y = $ .... °   [3]

c)

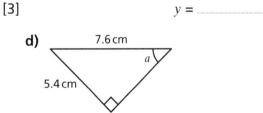

$z = $ .... °   [3]

d)

$a = $ .... °   [3]

Right-angled Triangles

4 The diagram shows the cross-section of a ramp.

Work out the angle θ of the ramp. Give your answer to 1 decimal place.

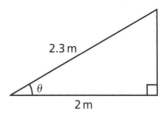

$\theta =$ _____ ° [3]

(PS) **5** ABCD is a rectangle.

Work out the size of angle CDB. Give your answer to 1 decimal place.

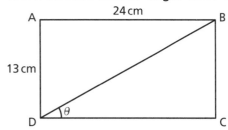

$\theta =$ _____ ° [3]

Total Marks _____ / 31

1 Complete the working to find the length of each lettered side.
Give your answers to 2 decimal places.

a)

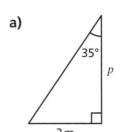

_____ $35° = \dfrac{2}{p}$

$p \times$ _____ $35° = 2$

$p = \dfrac{2}{\underline{\quad} 35°} =$ _____ m (2 d.p.)   [3]

b)

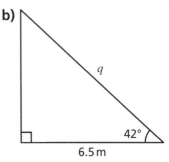

_____ $42° = \dfrac{6.5}{q}$

_____ $\times$ _____ $42° = 6.5$

$q = \dfrac{\underline{\quad}}{\underline{\quad}} =$ _____ m (2 d.p.)   [3]

72

c)

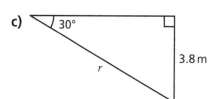

$$.......... 30° = \frac{\rule{2cm}{0.4pt}}{\rule{2cm}{0.4pt}}$$

$$.......... × .... 30° = 3.8$$

$$r = \frac{\rule{2cm}{0.4pt}}{\rule{1cm}{0.4pt}} = ... \text{ m (2 d.p.)} \qquad [3]$$

2 ABC is an isosceles triangle. D is the midpoint of BC.

AB = 7.5 cm   CD = 3 cm

a) Calculate angle CAD.

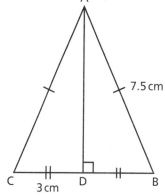

Angle CAD = ... ° [3]

b) Write down the size of angle BAD.

Angle BAD = ... ° [1]

c) What do the answers to parts a) and b) tell you about how the line AD intersects angle CAB?

....

.... [1]

3 **a)** Work out the height, h, of the triangle.
Give your answer to 2 decimal places.

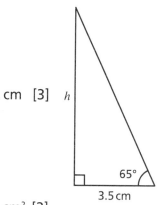

$h = $ .... cm [3]

b) Calculate the area, A, of the triangle.
Give your answer to 2 decimal places.

$A = $ .... cm² [2]

4 Find length x.

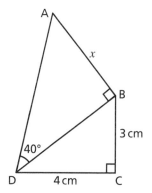

$x = $ .... cm [5]

Right-angled Triangles

(PS) **5** The diagram shows a ladder leaning against a wall.
The base of the ladder meets the ground at an angle of 75°.

a) Work out the length of the ladder.
Give your answer to 2 decimal places.

.... m [3]

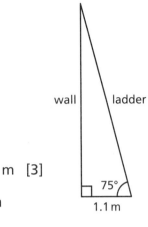

b) The same ladder is moved to a new position, so the top of it is 3.5 m above the ground.

Calculate the angle between the top of the ladder and the wall.
Give your answer to the nearest degree.

.... ° [3]

(MR) **6** This circle is centred on the origin and has radius 1 unit.
OPQ is a right-angled triangle.
Point P moves around the circle, anti-clockwise.

Work out the following, giving your answers to 2 decimal places where appropriate.

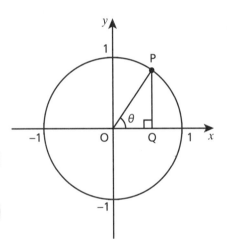

a) length OP

OP = ... unit(s) [1]

b) length PQ, when θ = 80°

PQ = ... unit(s) [2]

c) length OQ, when θ = 15°

OQ = ... unit(s) [2]

d) angle θ when PQ = 0.5

θ = ... ° [2]

e) angle θ when OQ = 0.5

θ = ... ° [2]

Total Marks .... / 39

.... / 31

.... / 31

.... / 39

How do you feel about these skills?

Green = Got it!
Orange = Nearly there
Red = Needs practice

Answers

Pages 4–9: Percentages

1.

| To find 10% divide by 10. | To find 1% divide by 100. |
| $50\% = \frac{1}{2}$ | $25\% = \frac{1}{4}$ |

1% = **2.4** [1]; 10% = **24** [1]; 15% = **36** [1]; 17% = **40.8** [1]; 25% = **60** [1]; 40% = **96** [1]; 50% = **120** [1]; 110% = **264** [1]

2.

Divide the numerator by the denominator to convert the fraction to a decimal. $\frac{2}{5} = 2 \div 5 = 0.4$

Multiply by 100% to convert the decimal to a percentage. $0.4 \times 100\% = 40\%$

a) $\frac{2}{5} = 0.4 = 40\%$ [1]

b) $\frac{1}{3} = 0.333... = 33.3\%$ [1]

c) $\frac{3}{8} = 0.375 = 37.5\%$ [1]

d) $\frac{11}{14} = 0.7857... = 78.6\%$ [1]

3.

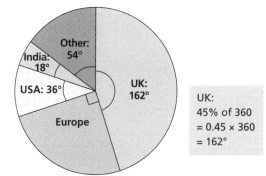

India: 18°
Other: 54°
USA: 36°
UK: 162°
Europe

UK:
45% of 360
= 0.45 × 360
= 162°

[5]

[1 mark for each correct sector]

4.

To write one number as a percentage of another, first write it as a fraction.

a) i) $\frac{95}{524} = 0.18129... = 18.1\%$ (1 d.p.) [1]

  ii) $\frac{46}{174} = 26.4\%$ (1 d.p.) [1]

  iii) $\frac{195}{350} = 55.7\%$ (1 d.p.) [1]

b) Yes it is an improvement. In the first week $\frac{95 + 293}{524}$
$= \frac{388}{524} = 74.0\%$ of trains were not late. [2]

[1 mark for 95 + 293 or 388 seen]

5. a) i) $\frac{3.5}{45} = 0.7777... = 7.8\%$ (1 d.p.) [1]

  ii) $\frac{27.8}{45} = 0.61777... = 61.8\%$ (1 d.p.) [1]

b) [1]

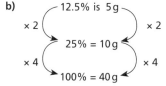

12.5% is 5 g
× 2
25% = 10 g
× 2
× 4
100% = 40 g
× 4

40 g [1]

c) $\frac{0.12}{6}$ [1]

$= 0.02 = 2\%$ [1]

1. a) 10% of 15 kg is 1.5 kg, 20% is 3 kg
120% is 15 + 3 = 18 kg [1]

b) 5.4 m [1]

c) 360 litres [1]

d) 0.84 km [1]

2. a) 10% of £25 is £2.50, 30% is £7.50
25 – 7.50 = £17.50 [1]

b) £26.60 [1]

c) £209.30 [1]

d) £10 500 [1]

3.

To increase by 20%, find 100 + 20 = 120%
To decrease by 15%, find 100 – 15 = 85%

a) To work out an amount after a 20% increase   × **1.2** [1]

b) To work out an amount after a 15% decrease   × **0.85** [1]

c) To work out an amount after a 4% increase   × **1.04** [1]

d) To work out an amount after a **25**% decrease   × 0.75 [1]

e) To work out an amount after a 2% decrease   × **0.98** [1]

f) To work out an amount after a 35% **increase**   × 1.35 [1]

g) To work out an amount after a **0.5**% increase   × 1.005 [2]

4.

To decrease by 22%, find 100% – 22% = 78%

a) £18 × 0.78 = £14.04 [1]

b) £512 × 0.78 = £399.36 [1]

c) 95p × 0.78 = 74.1p = 74p (to the nearest penny) [1]

d) £5 × 0.78 = £3.90 [1]

5. £10 500 × 0.87 = £9135 [1]

6.

	Old sugar content	New sugar content
Lemonade	9 g	9 × 0.82 = **7.38 g** [1]
Tonic	11 g	11 × 0.82 = **9.02 g** [1]
Apple drink	6.56 ÷ 0.82 = **8 g** [1]	6.56 g

7. 2021 → × **1.05** → 2022
   11 400 ← ÷ **1.05** ← **11 970**

   11 400 [1]

8. a) £319.20 ÷ 0.8 = £399 [1]

b) £340 ÷ 0.8 = £425 [1]

c) £440 ÷ 0.8 = £550 [1]

d) £656 ÷ 0.8 = £820 [1]

1.

Percentage change = $\frac{actual\ change}{original\ value} \times 100\%$

a) $\frac{0.07}{1.08} = 0.06481... = 6.5\%$ [1]

b) $\frac{0.18}{0.84} = 0.2142... = 21.4\%$ [1]

c) $\frac{0.14}{2.08} = 0.0673... = 6.7\%$ [1]

d) $\frac{0.08}{0.79} = 0.1012... = 10.1\%$ [1]

2. Percentage decrease in mass = $\frac{25}{200} = 12.5\%$ [1]
Percentage decrease in price = $\frac{0.15}{1.5} = 10\%$ [1]
The new price is not fair because it has not decreased as much as the mass has decreased. [1]

3. % reduction = $\frac{139}{399} = 0.3483... = 34.8\%$ (1 d.p.) [1]

4. % increase = $\frac{87}{210} = 0.4142... = 41.4\%$ (1 d.p.) [1]

5. % reduction = $\frac{20}{60} = 0.3333... = 33.3\%$ (1 d.p.) [1]

6. 12% deposit = £870

    Remainder to pay = £6380 [1]

    £6380 ÷ 20 = £319 per month [1]

7. 20% deposit = £219.80 [1]

    £219.80 + 10 × 90 = £1119.80 [1]

    % increase = $\frac{20.8}{1099}$ = 0.01892... = 1.9% (1 d.p.) [1]

Pages 10–17: Sequences, Equations and Formulae

1.

> To solve equations, use inverse operations and do the same to both sides.

a)
$4x = 20$, ÷ 4 ... ÷ 4, $x = 5$ [1]

b)
$9 + x = 12$, − 9 ... − 9, $x = 3$ [1]

c)
$\frac{x}{3} = 6$, × 3 ... × 3, $x = 18$ [1]

d) $x = 2$ [1]

e) $x = -3$ [1]

f) $x = -8$ [1]

g) $n = 9$ [1]

h) $y = \frac{7}{2} = 3\frac{1}{2}$ [1]

2. a)

A	B		C	
1	1	= 1	1	= 1
2	1 + 2	= 3	1 + 3	= 4
3	1 + 2 + 3	= 6	3 + 6	= 9
4	1 + 2 + 3 + 4	= 10	6 + 10	= 16
5	1 + 2 + 3 + 4 + 5	= 15	10 + 15	= 25

[3]

[1 mark for each correctly completed cell]

b) A Natural numbers [1]

    B Triangular numbers [1]

    C Square numbers [1]

3.

> Substitute the values given into the formula. This may give you an equation to solve.

Material	Density (g/cm³)	Mass (g)	Volume (cm³)
Steel	7.85 [1]	23.55	3
Mercury	13.59	163.08 [1]	12
Wood	1.5	450	300 [1]

4. a)
$s = \frac{d}{t}$, × t ... × t, $st = d$ [1]

    b)
$s = \frac{d}{t}$, × t ... × t, $st = d$, ÷ s ... ÷ s, $t = \frac{d}{s}$ [1]

5. a) $x + 9 = 14$ [1]

        $14 - x = 9$ [1]

        $x = 14 - 9$ [1]

    b) $6 + y = 23$ [1]

        $y = 23 - 6$ [1]

        $23 - y = 6$ [1]

c) $\frac{x}{5} = 3$ or $\frac{x}{3} = 5$ [1]

    $x = 5 \times 3$ or $x = 3 \times 5$ [1]

d) $4x = 32$ [1]

    $x = \frac{32}{4} = 8$ [1]

6. a) $A = bh$ [1]

    b) $h = \frac{A}{b}$ [1]

    c) $A = \frac{1}{2}bh$ [1]

    d) $b = \frac{2A}{h}$ [1]

1. a) $2x + 5 = 17$

        $2x = 12$ [1]

        $x = 6$ [1]

    b) $5y - 8 = 32$

        $5y = 40$ [1]

        $y = 8$ [1]

    c) $4a + 15 = 25$

        $4a = 10$ [1]

        $a = 2.5$ or $\frac{5}{2}$ [1]

    d) $19 - 2b = 13$

        $-2b = -6$ [1]

        $b = 3$ [1]

    e) $7 - 3c = 16$

        $-3c = 9$ [1]

        $c = -3$ [1]

    f) $8d + 11 = 5$

        $8d = -6$ [1]

        $d = -\frac{6}{8} = -\frac{3}{4} = -0.75$ [1]

2. a) $\frac{x}{3} + 5 = 7$

        $\frac{x}{3} = 2$ [1]

        $x = 6$ [1]

    b) $\frac{x}{4} - 5 = -8$

        $\frac{x}{4} = -3$ [1]

        $x = -12$ [1]

    c) $\frac{m+5}{3} = 9$

        $m + 5 = 27$ [1]

        $m = 22$ [1]

    d) $\frac{2x}{3} + 11 = 21$

        $\frac{2x}{3} = 10$ [1]

        $2x = 30$

        $x = 15$ [1]

    e) $19 - \frac{3x}{4} = 7$

        $-\frac{3x}{4} = -12$ [1]

        $-3x = -48$

        $x = 16$ [1]

    f) $\frac{5a-3}{2} = 16$

        $5a - 3 = 32$ [1]

        $5a = 35$

        $a = 7$ [1]

3. a) $C = 72n$ [1]

    b) $C = 0.72n$ [1]

4. $P = nr$ [1]

5. From the graph:
- the cost for 0 days is £80, so this is a fixed cost added on to the car hire
- the cost increases by £50 per day

The y-intercept is £80 and the gradient is 50.

$C = 5d + 80$ [2]

[1 mark for either 5d or 80]

6. a) $v = u + at$

$v = 0 + 5 \times 7 = 35$ m/s [1]

b) $15 = u - 2 \times 4$

$u = 23$ m/s [1]

c) $20 = 8 + 4a$

$12 = 4a$

$a = 3\,\text{m/s}^2$ [1]

d) $35.4 = 3 + 4.5t$

$32.4 = 4.5t$

$t = 7.2\,\text{s}$ [1]

7. a) $3x + 60° = 180°$ or $3x = 120°$ [1]

$x = 40°$ [1]

b) $3x + 9° = 180°$ or $3x = 171°$ [1]

$x = 57°$ [1]

8.

The formula for the angle sum S of an n-sided polygon is $S = 180(n - 2)$

a) $S = 180(11 - 2)$

$S = 1620°$ [1]

b) $3960° = 180(n - 2)$ [1]

$22 = n - 2$

$n = 24$ [1]

9.

Write an equation for nth term = 639, and solve. If n is a whole number, then 639 is a term in the sequence.

$14n - 19 = 639$ [1]

$14n = 658$

$n = \frac{658}{14} = 47$

639 is the 47th term in the sequence. [1]

10. a) $A = \frac{1}{2}(a + b)h$

$2A = (a + b)h$

$\frac{2A}{a + b} = h$ [1]

b) $A = \frac{1}{2}(a + b)h$

$\frac{2A}{h} = (a + b)$

$b = \frac{2A}{h} - a$ [1]

11. a) $y - mx = c$ [1]

b) $y - c = mx$

$\frac{y - c}{x} = m$ [1]

c) $c^2 - b^2 = a^2$

$\sqrt{c^2 - b^2} = a$ [1]

d) $x^2 = r^2y$ or $\frac{x}{r} = \sqrt{y}$

$\frac{x^2}{r^2} = y$ [1]

e) $\frac{A}{\pi} = r^2$

$\sqrt{\frac{A}{\pi}} = r$ [1]

f) $v^2 = u^2 + 2as$

$v = \sqrt{u^2 + 2as}$ [1]

g) $v^2 - 2as = u^2$

$u = \sqrt{v^2 - 2as}$ [1]

h) $\frac{v^2 - u^2}{2s} = a$ [1]

1. a) $7x = 3x + 28$

$4x = 28$ [1]

$x = 7$ [1]

b) $5x + 7 = 2x - 5$

$3x + 7 = -5$ [1]

$3x = -12$

$x = -4$ [1]

c) $2(x + 11) = 66$

$x + 11 = 33$ [1]

$x = 22$ [1]

Alternative method:

$2(x + 11) = 66$

$2x + 22 = 66$ [1]

$2x = 44$

$x = 22$ [1]

d) $5(2x + 7) = 3x + 14$

$10x + 35 = 3x + 14$

$7x + 35 = 14$ [1]

$7x = -21$

$x = -3$ [1]

e) $3(5x - 1) = 6(2x + 1)$

$15x - 3 = 12x + 6$

$3x - 3 = 6$ [1]

$3x = 9$

$x = 3$ [1]

Alternative method:

$3(5x - 1) = 6(2x + 1)$

$5x - 1 = 2(2x + 1)$

$5x - 1 = 4x + 2$ [1]

$x - 1 = 2$

$x = 3$ [1]

f) $7(x - 1) - 2(x - 6) = 60$

$7x - 7 - 2x + 12 = 60$

$5x + 5 = 60$ [1]

$5x = 55$

$x = 11$ [1]

2. a) B [1]

b) C [1]

c) A [1]

3.

$\div 3$ ⟨ 3 people take 2 hours ⟩ $\times 3$

1 person takes 6 hours

$\times n$ ⟨ ⟩ $\div n$

n people take $\frac{n}{6}$ hours

$t = \frac{n}{6}$ [1]

4. a) $\text{BMI} = \frac{\text{mass in kg}}{(\text{height in m})^2} = \frac{60}{1.65^2}$

$= 22$ (to the nearest whole number) [1]

b) $24 = \frac{76}{h^2}$

$24h^2 = 76$

$h = \sqrt{\frac{76}{24}}$ [1]

$= 1.78\,\text{m}$ (2 d.p.) [1]

5. a) $s = ut + \frac{1}{2}at^2$

   $s - \frac{1}{2}at^2 = ut$ [1]

   $\frac{s - \frac{1}{2}at^2}{t} = u$ or $\frac{s}{t} - \frac{1}{2}at = u$ [1]

   b) $s = ut + \frac{1}{2}at^2$

   $s - ut = \frac{1}{2}at^2$ [1]

   $2(s - ut) = at^2$

   $\frac{2(s - ut)}{t^2} = a$ [1]

6. a) Use 'opposite sides of a rectangle are equal' to find y.

   $2y + 5 = 5y - 4$ [1]

   $5 = 3y - 4$

   $9 = 3y$

   $3 = y$ [1]

   $2y + 5 = 6 + 5 = 11$ or $5y - 4 = 15 - 4 = 11$ [1]

   Perimeter $= 11 + 20 + 11 + 20 = 62\,\text{cm}$ [1]

   b) Area $= lw = 20 \times 11 = 220\,\text{cm}^2$ [1]

7. Rearrange the equation for Line L_2 into the form $y = mx + c$ so you can compare the gradients.

   Line L_2 $2y - 6x + 1 = 0$

   $2y = 6x - 1$

   $y = 3x - \frac{1}{2}$ [1]

   Line L_1 has equation $y = 3x - 4$

   Lines L_1 and L_2 are parallel because they both have the same gradient, 3. [1]

Pages 18–23: Similarity, Congruence and Scaling

1. a) F, H, I [2]

   [1 mark for two correct]

   b) D, J [2]

   [1 mark for one correct and no incorrect answers]

   c) Shape drawn identical to shape C, in any orientation. [1]

   Congruent means 'exactly the same shape and size'. Congruent shapes may be facing in different directions.

2. a) Scale factor 2 [1]

   b) similar [1]

3.

   [1]

   In an enlargement, all the lengths of the original shape are multiplied by the scale factor.

4.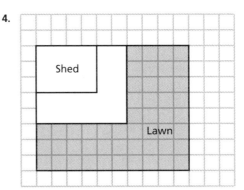

   [4 marks for correct diagram; 1 mark for correct length and width of garden; 1 mark for correct length and width of shed; 1 mark for one correct length of either 6 cm or 4 cm on the lawn]

5. Square 4 [1]; Rectangle 2 [1]; Parallelogram 2 [1]; Equilateral triangle 3 [1]

1. X and Y [1]

   Congruent triangles have the same angles and one equal pair of corresponding sides.

2. a) Enlargement centre (0, 0), scale factor 4 [2]

   [1 mark for either scale factor or centre correct]

   b) Enlargement centre (0, 0), scale factor $\frac{1}{4}$ [2]

   [1 mark for either scale factor or centre correct]

   To describe an enlargement, state the scale factor and the centre of the enlargement.

3. a) $6 \times x = 15$

   Scale factor $= 2.5$ [1]

   b) $2.5 \times 2 = 5\,\text{cm}$ [1]

4. a) $1 : 50$ $\times 9$ ⟶ $\times 9$ $9 : 450$

   9 cm [2]

   [1 mark for comparing 50 and 450 if final answer is incorrect]

   b) $1 : 50$ $\times 2.8$ ⟶ $\times 2.8$ $2.8 : 140$

   1.4 m [2]

   [1 mark for multiplying 50 by 2.8 if final answer is incorrect]

5. a) PQ = 5 cm on the diagram

   5 cm represents 25 m, so scale is 1 cm represents 5 m [1]

   b) QR = 4.3 cm on the diagram

   Scale is 1 cm represents 5 m

   4.3 cm represents $5 \times 4.3 = 21.5\,\text{m}$ [1]

   [1 mark for correct calculation based on inaccurate measurement of 4.2 cm or 4.4 cm]

1. $20\,000\,\text{cm} = 200\,\text{m}$ [1]

2. $25\,000\,\text{cm} = 250\,\text{m}$

   $12 \times 250\,\text{m} = 3000\,\text{m} = 3\,\text{km}$ [2]

   [1 mark for multiplying 12×250 or $12 \times 25\,000$ correctly if final answer is incorrect]

3. a) Width: 120% of 20 = 1.2 × 20 = 24 cm [1]

   Length: 120% of 25 = 1.2 × 25 = 30 cm [1]

   b) Width: 70% of 20 = 0.7 × 20 = 14 cm [1]

   Length: 70% of 25 = 0.7 × 25 = 17.5 cm [1]

4.

   $\div 5.5 \Big($ 5.5 : 33 000 $\Big) \div 5.5$

   1 : 6000 [2]

   [If final answer is incorrect, 1 mark for writing correct scale in different format, e.g. 1 cm represents 6000 cm, or 1 cm represents 60 m]

5. a) Scale factor of enlargement from A to B:

   4 × ? = 7, scale factor = $\frac{7}{4}$ (or 1.75) [1]

   $x = 3 \times \frac{7}{4} = \frac{21}{4} = 5.25$ cm or $5\frac{1}{4}$ cm [1]

   b) y × 1.75 = 8.75 or 8.75 ÷ 1.75 [1]

   $y = 5$ cm [1]

6. No [1]

   Explanation such as: The side lengths of the grey rectangle are not the same multiples of the side lengths of the white triangle. Doubling the lengths of the white rectangle gives a rectangle of 12 cm by 10 cm, but the grey rectangle is only 11 cm by 10 cm. [1]

Pages 24–30: Applications of Graphs

1. a)

Number of hours, h	Cost (£)
0 < h ⩽ 1	26
1 < h ⩽ 2	34
2 < h ⩽ 4	40
4 < h ⩽ 6	48

[3]

   [1 mark for each cell correctly completed]

   b)

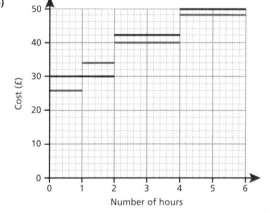

[2]

   [1 mark for one cost correctly shown]

   c) Small car for 5 hours costs £48 and larger car for 2 hours costs £30, giving total £78. [1]

   Small car for 2 hours costs £34 and larger car for 5 hours costs £50, giving total £84. [1]

   Mr Smith should hire the small car and Mrs Smith the larger car. [1]

2. a)

	Fixed cost	Price per mile (after the fixed cost)
Company A	£4 up to 1 mile	£1.50
Company B	£6 up to 2 miles	£1.00

[2]

   [1 mark for each column correctly completed]

   b) Cost is £5 + £1.25 × 8 [1]

   = £5 + £10 = £15 [1]

   c)

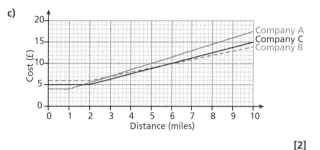

[2]

   [1 mark for fixed cost line correct; 1 mark for line from (2, 5) to (10, 15)]

   d) Company A [1]

   e) A journey of over 10 miles is cheapest using Company **B**. [1]

   The costs with Company A and Company B is exactly the same for a journey of **3** miles. [1]

   A journey of 4 miles is cheapest with Company **C**. [1]

1. a) The train sets off again [1]

   b) 62.5 km [1]

   c) Any answer from 3.30 pm to 4 pm [1]

   d) A False [1]

   Including the return journey, the total distance was 300 km.

   B True [1]

   The steepest part of the graph is on the return.

   C True [1]

   The stop was from 2.00 pm to 2.30 pm.

   D False [1]

   The line is steeper so faster on first part.

   E False [1]

   As a curve, the speed is changing (slowing down)

2. a) Arron [1]

   b) 45 s [accept any answer from 40 to 50 s] [1]

3. a) 2 s [1]

   b) $\frac{20}{50}$ or $\frac{2}{5}$ [1]

   c) $\frac{2}{5}$ of 8 [1]

   = 3.2 m [1]

4.

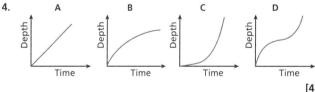

[4]

   [1 mark for each]

5. a)

Number of years	0	1	2	3	4
Number of fish	40	80	160	320	640

[2]

   [1 mark for at least two correct values]

b)

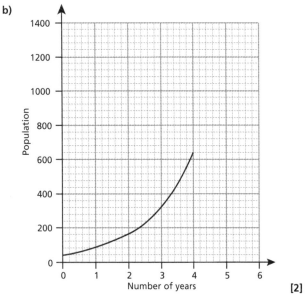

[2]
[1 mark for points plotted correctly;
1 mark for a smooth curve]

c) 4.6 years (approx.) [2]

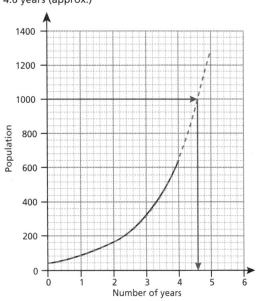

[1 mark for extending the curve as shown;
1 mark for reading off at 1000, giving approx. 4.6 years]

1. a)

Round	1	2	3	4	5	6
Number of players	256	128	64	32	16	8

[2]

[1 mark for at least three correct values]

b)

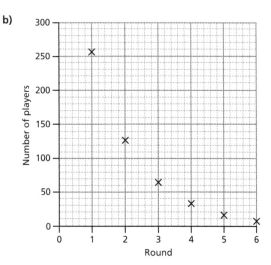

[2]

[1 mark for at least three correctly plotted values]

c) You cannot read off the number of players between rounds so it is not possible to read off at intermediate points. [1]

d) 8 [1]

2. a)

Number of years	0	1	2	3	4	5	6
Value of investment (£)	1000	1050	1102.50	1157.63	1215.51	1276.28	1340.10

[3]

[2 marks for at least three correct values; 1 mark for £1102.50]

b)

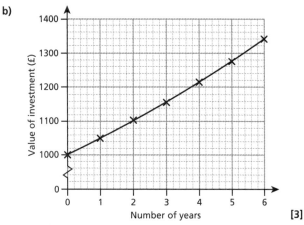

[3]

[2 marks for at least four correct points plotted;
1 mark for at least two correct points plotted]

c) A False [1]   B True [1]
   C True [1]   D False [1]

   A linear graph is a straight line graph.

d) 1000×1.05^{10} [1]
   = £1628.89 or £1628.90 [1]

Pages 31–37: Pythagoras' Theorem

1. The longest side [1]

2. a) a [1] b) e [1] c) h [1] d) l [1] e) o [1] f) r [1]

   hyp ◺ b Pythagoras' Theorem:
        a $a^2 + b^2 = hyp^2$

3. a) x cannot be 5 cm because the longest side in the triangle is 4 cm [1]

b) Jamie has used x as the hypotenuse [1]

c) $x^2 + 3^2 = 4^2$ [1]

$x^2 = 16 - 9 = 7$ [1]

$x = \sqrt{7} = 2.6\,\text{cm}$ [1]

> x is one of the shorter sides so square the other sides then subtract. Square root at the end.

4. a) $x^2 = 4^2 + 6^2 = 52$ [1]

$x = \sqrt{52} = 7.2\,\text{cm}$ [1]

b) $x^2 + 7^2 = 11^2$ so $x^2 = 121 - 49 = 72$ [1]

$x = \sqrt{72} = 8.5\,\text{cm}$ [1]

c) $x^2 + 9^2 = 14^2$ so $x^2 = 196 - 81 = 115$ [1]

$x = \sqrt{115} = 10.7\,\text{cm}$ [1]

d) $x^2 + 5^2 = 16^2$ so $x^2 = 256 - 25 = 231$ [1]

$x = \sqrt{231} = 15.2\,\text{cm}$ [1]

e) $x^2 = 3^2 + 10^2 = 109$ [1]

$x = \sqrt{109} = 10.4\,\text{cm}$ [1]

f) $x^2 + 8^2 = 18^2$ so $x^2 = 324 - 64 = 260$ [1]

$x = \sqrt{260} = 16.1\,\text{cm}$ [1]

1. Let d = diagonal, $d^2 = 48^2 + 36^2 = 3600$ [1]

$d = \sqrt{3600} = 60$ inches [1]

2. Let x = hypotenuse, $x^2 = 62^2 + 50^2 = 6344$ [1]

$x = \sqrt{6344} = 79.65\,\text{km}$ [1]

3.

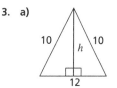

Camp **[1 mark for diagram]**

$x^2 = 3.6^2 + 6.1^2 = 50.17$ [1]

$x = \sqrt{50.17} = 7.1\,\text{km}$ [1]

Total distance walked = 3.6 + 6.1 + 7.1
= 16.8 km [1]

4. a) $x^2 = 3.7^2 + 1.9^2 = 17.3$ [1]

Ladder length $x = \sqrt{17.3} = 4.16\,\text{m}$ [1]

b)

New ladder length = 4.16 + 0.64
= 4.8 m [1]

$y^2 + 1.9^2 = 4.8^2$

so $y^2 = 23.04 - 3.61 = 19.43$ [1]

$y = \sqrt{19.43} = 4.4\,\text{m}$ [1]

Ladder now reaches 4.4 m up the wall.

5. a) $a = 5$ [1]

b) $b = 40$ [1]

c) $c = 29$ [1]

1.

$x^2 = 15^2 + 20^2 = 625$ [1]

$x = \sqrt{625} = 25\,\text{m}$ [1]

$y^2 + 24^2 = 25^2$ so $y^2 = 625 - 576 = 49$ [1]

$y = \sqrt{49} = 7\,\text{m}$ [1]

2.

$h^2 + 8^2 = 17^2$ so $h^2 = 289 - 64 = 225$ [1]

$h = \sqrt{225} = 15\,\text{cm}$ [1]

Area of triangle P = $\frac{8 \times 15}{2} = 60\,\text{cm}^2$ [1]

Area of triangle Q = $\frac{11 \times 10}{2} = 55\,\text{cm}^2$ [1]

Triangle P has the larger area by 5 cm² [1]

3. a)

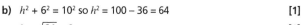 [1]

b) $h^2 + 6^2 = 10^2$ so $h^2 = 100 - 36 = 64$ [1]

$h = \sqrt{64} = 8\,\text{cm}$ [1]

c) $\frac{12 \times 8}{2}$ **[1]** = 48 cm² **[1]**

4. $\frac{\text{base} \times \text{height}}{2}$ = area, so $\frac{\text{base} \times 24}{2} = 84$, so base = 7 m [1]

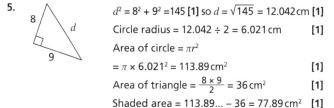

$x^2 = 7^2 + 24^2 = 625$ **[1]**, so $x = \sqrt{625} = 25$ [1]

Perimeter = 7 + 24 + 25 = 56 m [1]

Cost = (56 ÷ 2) × 5.67 **[1]** = £158.76 **[1]**

5.

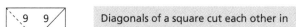

$d^2 = 8^2 + 9^2 = 145$ **[1]** so $d = \sqrt{145} = 12.042\,\text{cm}$ **[1]**

Circle radius = 12.042 ÷ 2 = 6.021 cm [1]

Area of circle = πr^2

= $\pi \times 6.021^2 = 113.89\,\text{cm}^2$ [1]

Area of triangle = $\frac{8 \times 9}{2} = 36\,\text{cm}^2$ [1]

Shaded area = 113.89... − 36 = 77.89 cm² [1]

6.

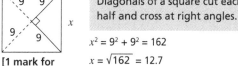

[1 mark for diagram]

> Diagonals of a square cut each other in half and cross at right angles.

$x^2 = 9^2 + 9^2 = 162$ [1]

$x = \sqrt{162} = 12.7$ [1]

Lawn perimeter = 12.7 × 4 = 51 m [1]

7.

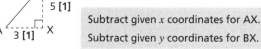

$AB^2 = 3^2 + 5^2 = 34$ [1]

$AB = \sqrt{34}$ units [1]

> Subtract given x coordinates for AX.
> Subtract given y coordinates for BX.

8.

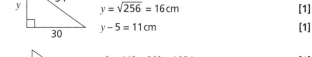

$y^2 + 30^2 = 34^2$ so $y = 256$ [1]

$y = \sqrt{256} = 16\,\text{cm}$ [1]

$y - 5 = 11\,\text{cm}$ [1]

$x^2 = 11^2 + 30^2 = 1021$ [1]

$x = \sqrt{1021}\,\text{cm}$ [1]

9. No because the square root of $24^2 + 19^2$ is not equal to 29 **[1]** so it is not a right-angled triangle. **[1]**

Pages 38–41: Fractions

1. a) $0.7 = \frac{7}{10}$ [1]

b) $0.19 = \frac{19}{100}$ [1]

c) $0.321 = \frac{321}{1000}$ [1]

d) $0.8 = \frac{8}{10} = \frac{4}{5}$ [1]

e) $0.85 = \frac{85}{100} = \frac{17}{20}$ [1]

f) $0.852 = \frac{852}{1000} = \frac{213}{250}$ [1]

g) $0.06 = \frac{6}{100} = \frac{3}{50}$ [1]

h) $0.004 = \frac{4}{1000} = \frac{1}{250}$ [1]

2.

Fraction	$\frac{2}{5}$	$\frac{1}{8}$ [1]	$\frac{3}{4}$ [1]	$\frac{7}{10}$	$\frac{19}{20}$ [1]	$\frac{5}{8}$ [1]	$\frac{11}{20}$
Decimal	0.4 [1]	0.125	0.75 [1]	0.7 [1]	0.95 [1]	0.625	0.55 [1]
Percentage	40%	12.5% [1]	75%	70% [1]	95%	62.5% [1]	55% [1]

3. a) 12 minutes $= \frac{12}{60} = \frac{1}{5} = 0.2$ hours [1]

b) 0.5 hours [1]

c) 0.6 hours [1]

d) 0.8 hours [1]

4.

> Compare pairs of fractions, or convert them all to fractions with common denominator 60.

$\frac{8}{15}$ $\frac{2}{3}$ $\frac{3}{4}$ $\frac{5}{6}$ $\frac{11}{12}$ [3]

[2 marks for four in the correct order; 1 mark for three in the correct order]

---

1. a) 1 hour + 0.2 × 60 minutes = 1 hour 12 minutes [1]

b) 3 hours 24 minutes [1]

c) 5 hours 45 minutes [1]

d) 2 hours 42 minutes [1]

2. 35 people under 16

80 people 65 or over

25 people are between 16 and 59 [2]

[1 mark for correct number for one of the age groups]

3. $\frac{1}{5} \times \frac{2}{3} = \frac{2}{15}$ [1]

4. $1 - \frac{5}{9} = \frac{4}{9}$

12 students are $\frac{4}{9}$ of the class; 3 students are $\frac{1}{9}$ of the class

There are 3 × 9 = 27 students in the class [2]

[1 mark for '12 students are $\frac{4}{9}$ of the class' or '3 students are $\frac{1}{9}$ of the class']

5. a) $\frac{5}{7}$ [1]

b) 8 sweets are $\frac{2}{7}$ of the total; 4 sweets are $\frac{1}{7}$ of the total

There are 4 × 7 = 28 sweets [2]

[1 mark for '8 sweets are $\frac{2}{7}$ of the total' or '4 sweets are $\frac{1}{7}$ of the total']

6. a) Pottery club total is 35 students; 11 are from Year 9

$\frac{11}{35}$ [1]

b) Year 7 students total 40; 8 go to Drama

$\frac{8}{40} = \frac{1}{5}$ [1]

c) Total of Key Stage 3 students is 122; 48 go to Choir

$\frac{48}{122} = \frac{24}{61}$ [1]

d) 48 students go to Choir; 26 are in Year 8 or 9

$\frac{26}{48} = \frac{13}{24}$ [1]

e) Choir $\frac{19}{48} = 0.3950...$, Drama $\frac{14}{39} = 0.3589...$, Pottery $\frac{14}{35} = 0.4$

Pottery has the highest proportion of Year 8 students [2]

[1 mark for one correct proportion (fraction or decimal)]

---

1. a)

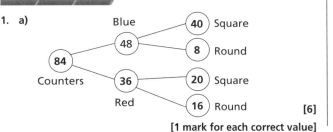

[6]

[1 mark for each correct value]

---

b) $\frac{8 + 16}{84} = \frac{24}{84} = \frac{2}{7}$ [1]

[1 mark for correct fraction, whether simplified or not]

2. a) $\frac{3}{5}x^2$ [1]

b) $2x + \frac{6}{5}x = 3\frac{1}{5}x$ [1]

c) $2x + 6 \times \frac{3}{5}x = 2x + \frac{18}{5}x = 2x + 3\frac{3}{5}x$ [1]

$= 5\frac{3}{5}x$ [1]

3. a) $\frac{\text{length AB}}{\text{length PQ}} = \frac{5}{8}$ [1]

b) $x = \frac{5}{8} \times 4 = 2.5$ cm [1]

c) $\frac{\text{area ABC}}{\text{area PQR}} = \frac{\frac{1}{2} \times 2.5 \times 5}{\frac{1}{2} \times 4 \times 8} = \frac{6.25}{16}$ [1] $= \frac{25}{64}$ [1]

> A fraction must have integer numerator and denominator.

4. Average speed $= \frac{\text{total distance}}{\text{total time}}$

Time $= \frac{\text{distance}}{\text{speed}} = \frac{154}{70} = 2.2$ hours [1]

Distance = speed × time = 60 × 3.25 = 195 miles [1]

Average speed $= \frac{\text{total distance}}{\text{total time}} = \frac{154 + 195}{2.2 + 3.25}$

$= 64.036... = 64$ mph (to the nearest integer) [1]

Pages 42–48: Probability

1.

[4]

[1 mark for A in correct position; 1 mark for B in correct position; 1 mark for C in correct position; 1 mark for D and E in correct positions]

2. There are 4 triangles (A), 2 circles (B), 3 squares and 3 pentagons totalling 6 shapes (C), 3 squares (D), no shapes with exactly two lines of symmetry (E) or P(A) $= \frac{4}{12}$, P(B) $= \frac{2}{12}$, P(C) $= \frac{6}{12}$, P(D) $= \frac{3}{12}$, P(E) = 0 [1]

So the correct order is E, B, D A, C [1]

3. a) 2, 4, 6 and 8 are the even numbers so P(even) $= \frac{4}{8} = \frac{1}{2}$ [1]

b) 2, 3, 5 and 7 are the prime numbers so P(prime) $= \frac{4}{8} = \frac{1}{2}$ [1]

c) 3 and 6 are the multiples of 3 so P(multiple of 3) $= \frac{2}{8} = \frac{1}{4}$ [1]

4. As the coin is fair, it is equally likely to land on Head or Tail each time so P(Head) $= \frac{1}{2}$ [1]

5. a) P(1) $= \frac{2}{8} = \frac{1}{4}$ [1]

b) P(2) $= \frac{3}{8}$ [1]

c) P(3) $= \frac{1}{8}$ [1]

d) P(4) $= \frac{2}{8} = \frac{1}{4}$ [1]

e) $\frac{1}{4}$ of 80 = 20 [1]

6. a) $\frac{74}{100}$ [1]

b) 40 out of 50 is $\frac{80}{100}$ or 74 ÷ 2 = 37 [1]

So, better [1]

7. a) Probably biased as would expect all frequencies to be approximately same if fair. [1]

b) Carry out more rolls of the dice. [1]

c) $\frac{18}{90}$ or $\frac{1}{5}$ [1]

d 19 + 15 + 12 or 46 [1]

$\frac{19 + 15 + 12}{90} = \frac{46}{90}$ or $\frac{23}{45}$ [1]

1.

Outcome	Probability of outcome occurring (p)	Probability of outcome not occurring ($1 - p$)
A	$\frac{1}{2}$	$\frac{1}{2}$ [1]
B	$\frac{1}{4}$	$\frac{3}{4}$ [1]
C	$\frac{1}{5}$	$\frac{4}{5}$ [1]
D	$\frac{3}{5}$	$\frac{2}{5}$ [1]
E	0.3	0.7 [1]
F	0.9	0.1 [1]
G	0.41	0.59 [1]
H	0.65	0.35 [1]

2. a) $\frac{10}{20}$ or $\frac{1}{2}$ [1]
b) $\frac{9}{20}$ [1]
c) $\frac{10}{20}$ or $\frac{1}{2}$ [1]
d) $\frac{5}{20}$ or $\frac{1}{4}$ [1]
e) $\frac{15}{20}$ or $\frac{3}{4}$ [1]
f) $\frac{8}{20}$ or $\frac{2}{5}$ [1]

The prime numbers are 2, 3, 5, 7, 11, 13, 17 and 19.

3. Number of red counters is $\frac{1}{5}$ of 40 $= \frac{1}{5} \times 40 = 8$ [1]
Number of blue counters is 40 – 8 = 32 [1]

Alternative method:
P(Blue) $= 1 - \frac{1}{5}$
$= \frac{4}{5}$ [1]
Number of blue counters is $\frac{4}{5}$ of 40 $= \frac{4}{5} \times 40 = 32$ [1]

4. a)

Total score	1	2	3	4	5	6
1	2	3	4	5	6	7
2	3	4	5	6	7	8
3	4	5	6	7	8	9
4	5	6	7	8	9	10
5	6	7	8	9	10	11
6	7	8	9	10	11	12

[2]
[1 mark for at least two correct rows]

b) 7 [1]
c) $\frac{3}{36}$ or $\frac{1}{12}$ [1]
d) $\frac{30}{36}$ or $\frac{5}{6}$ [1]
e) $\frac{33}{36}$ or $\frac{11}{12}$ [1]

5. a) Not correct as there could have been other colours that were not chosen [1]
b) 60 ÷ 20 = 3, so 15 × 3 or $\frac{15}{20} \times 60$ or $\frac{3}{4} \times 60$ [1]
= 45 [1]

6. a) 30p, 60p, 70p, £1.10, £1.20, £1.50, £2.10, £2.20, £2.50, £3 [2]
[1 mark for at least six correct amounts]
b) P(more than £2) $= \frac{4}{10}$ or $\frac{2}{5}$ or 4 ways [1]
P(less than £2) $= \frac{6}{10}$ or $\frac{3}{5}$ or 6 ways
So less than £2 is more likely [1]

7. a) Yes [1] b) No [1] c) Yes [1] d) No [1] e) No [1]
f) No [1] g) Yes [1] h) Yes [1] i) Yes [1] j) No [1]
k) No [1] l) Yes [1]

---

1. a) $\frac{8}{18} = \frac{4}{9}$ [1]
b) There are now 18 + 6 = 24 counters in the bag [1]
$\frac{1}{3}$ of 24 = 8 [1]
So 0 blue counters added [1]

2. a) $\frac{1}{6}$ [1]
b) With one dice, roll a 4 [1]
With two dice, roll 1 and 3, or 2 and 2, or 3 and 1 [1]
c) If Ali rolls one dice, his probability of winning is $\frac{1}{6}$ [1]
If he rolls two dice, his probability of winning is $\frac{5}{36}$
(1 and 5, 2 and 4, 3 and 3, 4 and 2, 5 and 1) [1]
So to win in one go, he should roll one dice [1]

Ali will definitely still be in the game if he rolls one dice.

3. a)

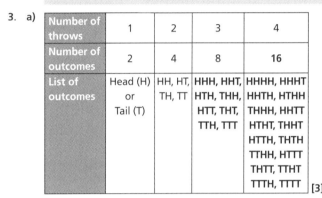

Number of throws	1	2	3	4
Number of outcomes	2	4	8	16
List of outcomes	Head (H) or Tail (T)	HH, HT, TH, TT	HHH, HHT, HTH, THH, HTT, THT, TTH, TTT	HHHH, HHHT, HHTH, HTHH, THHH, HHTT, HTHT, THHT, HTTH, THTH, TTHH, HTTT, THTT, TTHT, TTTH, TTTT

[3]
[1 mark for each correct cell]

b) 16 × 2 = 32 [1]

4. a)

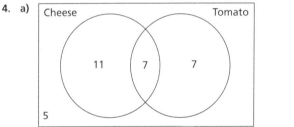

[4]
[1 mark for each correct value]

b) $\frac{7}{30}$ [1]

Pages 49–51: Simplifying Expressions, Expanding Brackets and Factorising

1. a) $x(x + 4)$ [1]
$= x^2 + 4x$ [1]
b) $\frac{1}{2} \times 2x \times (x - 7)$ or $x(x - 7)$ [1]
$= x^2 - 7x$ [1]

2. a) $5(2 + 3x)$ [1]
b) $7(4 - 3y)$ [1]
c) $c(8 + c)$ [1]
d) $d(6 - d)$ [1]
e) $x(x + w)$ [1]
f) $y(y - x)$ [1]

1. a) $10x(y + z)$ [1]
b) $6m(2n - 3p)$ [1]
c) $8c(3 + 2c)$ [1]

d) $12d(1 - 3d)$ [1]

e) $9x(2x + 3w)$ [1]

f) $2y(3y - x)$ [1]

2. $3x$ cm [1]

3. a) $x^2 + 8x + 5x + 40$ [1]

$= x^2 + 13x + 40$ [1]

b) $y^2 - 3y + 2y - 6$ [1]

$= y^2 - y - 6$ [1]

c) $z^2 + 3z - 4z - 12$ [1]

$= z^2 - z - 12$ [1]

d) $w^2 - 2w - 6w + 12$ [1]

$= w^2 - 8w + 12$ [1]

1. Boxes should be joined as follows:

$x^2 - 16$	to	$(x - 4)(x + 4)$
$x^2 - 8x + 16$	to	$(x - 4)(x - 4)$
$x^2 - 1$	to	$(x - 1)(x + 1)$
$x^2 + 8x + 16$	to	$(x + 4)(x + 4)$
$x^2 - 50x + 625$	to	$(x - 25)(x - 25)$
$x^2 + 6x - 16$	to	$(x - 2)(x + 8)$
$x^2 - 25$	to	$(x - 5)(x + 5)$	[5]

[4 marks for four correct; 3 marks for three correct; 2 marks for two correct; 1 mark for one correct]

2. Area of square is $(x + 3)(x + 3)$ [1]

$= x^2 + 6x + 9$ [1]

3. Area of shaded shape $= (x + 2)(x + 5) - 1(x + 1)$

$= x^2 + 7x + 10 - x - 1$ [1]

$= x^2 + 6x + 9$ [1]

4. $(x + 2)(x + 3)(x - 4) = (x^2 + 3x + 2x + 6)(x - 4)$

or $(x^2 + 5x + 6)(x - 4)$ [1]

$= x^3 - 4x^2 + 5x^2 - 20x + 6x - 24$ [1]

$= x^3 + x^2 - 14x - 24$ [1]

5. a) Volume $= 4x(x + 1)(x - 1)$ [1]

$= 4x(x^2 - 1) = 4x^3 - 4x$ [1]

b) Volume $= 4(2)^3 - 4(2)$ [1]

$= 32 - 8 = 24\,\text{cm}^3$ [1]

Alternative method:

Length $= 4(2) = 8$ cm, width $= 2 - 1 = 1$ cm

Height $= 2 + 1 = 3$ cm [1]

Volume $= 8 \times 1 \times 3 = 24\,\text{cm}^3$ [1]

Pages 52–56: Standard Form

1. a) $1\,000\,000$ [1]   **b)** $100\,000$ [1]   **c)** 100 [1]

2. a) $10^{-2} = \frac{1}{100} = 0.01$ [1]

b) $10^{-4} = \frac{1}{10\,000} = 0.0001$ [1]

c) $10^{-1} = \frac{1}{10} = 0.1$ [1]

d) $10^{-3} = \frac{1}{1000} = 0.001$ [1]

3.

When you multiply powers of the same number, you add the powers (indices). 'Indices' is another word for powers.

a) $10^2 \times 10^3 = 10^{2+3} = 10^5$ [1]

b) $10^{-2} \times 10^3 = 10^{-2+3} = 10^1$ [1]

$= 10$ [1]

c) 10^{-3} [1]

d) 10^0 [1]

$= 1$ [1]

4.

When you divide powers of the same number, you subtract the powers (indices).

a) $10^5 \div 10^3 = 10^{5-3} = 10^2$ [1]   **b)** 10^2 [1]

c) 10^{-2} [1]   **d)** 10^0 [1] $= 1$ [1]

5. $4.2 \times \mathbf{10}$ [1]; $4200 \times \frac{1}{100}$ [1]; 420×0.1 [1]; $42\,000 \times \mathbf{0.001}$ [1]; $0.042 \times \mathbf{1000}$ [1]; 0.42×10^2 [1]

6. Boxes joined as follows:

giga to 10^9

nano to 10^{-9}

mega to 10^6

milli to 10^{-3}

kilo to 10^3

micro to 10^{-6} [4]

[3 marks for three correct; 2 marks for two correct; 1 mark for one correct]

1. a) $8.1 \times 10^3 = 8.1 \times 1000$

$= 8100$ [1]

b) $450\,000$ [1]

c) $1\,200\,000$ [1]

d) 506 [1]

e) $790\,000\,000$ [1]

f) $31\,500$ [1]

2. a) 5.2×10^3 [1]

b) 3.5×10^2 [1]

c) 4.07×10^3 [1]

d) 1.25×10^5 [1]

e) 2.7×10^1 **[accept 2.7×10]** [1]

f) 2.005×10^6 [1]

3.

A number in standard form is written as $A \times 10^n$ where $1 \leqslant A < 10$ and n is an integer (positive or negative whole number).

a) 37×10^4 is not in standard form because 37 is not a number between 1 and 10. [1]

b) $37 \times 10^4 = 3.7 \times \mathbf{10} \times 10^4$ [1]

$= 3.7 \times 10^5$ [1]

4. a) $2.6 \times 10 \times 10^3 = 2.6 \times 10^4$ [1]

b) $5.1 \times 10^2 \times 10^4 = 5.1 \times 10^6$ [1]

c) $3.07 \times 10^2 \times 10^2 = 3.07 \times 10^4$ [1]

d) $3.32 \times 10 \times 10^4 = 3.32 \times 10^5$ [1]

5. a) 0.26×10^3 is not in standard form because 0.26 is not a number between 1 and 10. [1]

b) $0.26 \times 10^3 = 2.6 \times \frac{1}{10} \times 10^3$ [1]

$= 2.6 \times 10^{-1} \times 10^3$ [1]

$= 2.6 \times 10^{\mathbf{2}}$ [1]

6. First order the numbers by their powers of 10, smallest power first.

8.2×10^3 3.7×10^3 4.5×10^5 3.7×10^5 1.6×10^6

Then compare numbers with the same power of 10.

3.7×10^3 8.2×10^3 3.7×10^5 4.5×10^5 1.6×10^6 **[3]**

[2 marks for four in the correct order;
1 mark for three in the correct order]

7. giga = 10^9

32×10^9 **[1]**

$= 3.2 \times 10 \times 10^9$

$= 3.2 \times 10^{10}$ **[1]**

8. 1 GB = 10^9 bytes   1 MB = 10^6 bytes

$\frac{10^9}{10^6} = 10^3$

1 GB is 10^3 or 1000 times bigger than 1 MB **[1]**

1. a) $2 \times 0.01 = 0.02$ **[1]**

b) 0.000035 **[1]**

c) 0.16 **[1]**

d) 0.00072 **[1]**

e) 0.00000507 **[1]**

f) 0.00004 **[1]**

2. a) $5 \times 0.001 = 5 \times 10^{-3}$ **[1]**

b) 6.04×10^{-1} **[1]**

c) 2.5×10^{-4} **[1]**

d) 5.16×10^{-5} **[1]**

e) 3×10^{-3} **[1]**

f) 7.1×10^{-6} **[1]**

3. $0.052 \times 10^{-5} = 5.2 \times 10^{-2} \times 10^{-5}$ **[1]**

$= 5.2 \times 10^{-7}$ **[1]**

4. a) 1.7×10^7 metres **[1]**

b) 2.095×10^{11} metres **[1]**

c) 2.75×10^{-10} metres **[1]**

5. a) Mercury **[1]**   b) Neptune **[1]**   c) Jupiter **[1]**

d) Mercury **[1]**   e) Neptune **[1]**

6. a) $2 \times 3.35 \times 10^{25} = 6.7 \times 10^{25}$ **[1]**

b) $5 \times 3.35 \times 10^{25} = 16.75 \times 10^{25}$ **[1]**

$= 1.675 \times 10^{26}$ **[1]**

7. $120 \times 1 \times 10^{-3} = 1.2 \times 10^{-1}$g **[1]**

8. a) 7.753×10^9 **[1]**

b) $\frac{7.753 \times 10^9}{1.7 \times 10^9} = 4.56...$ **[1]**

The 2020 population was approximately 4.56 times greater than the 1920 population. **[1]**

Pages 57–64: Using Algebraic Graphs

1. a) $y = 2x - 1$

x	−2	−1	0	1	2
y	−5	−3	−1	1	3

[1]

b) $y = -x + 2$

x	−2	−1	0	1	2
y	4	3	2	1	0

[1]

c)

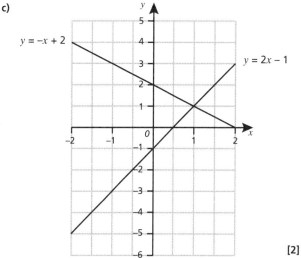

[2]

[1 mark for each correct line]

2.

Equation	Gradient	Coordinates of y-intercept
$y = 2x + 4$	2	(0, 4)
$y = 3x$	3	(0, 0)
$y = -4$	0	(0, −4)
$y = 5 - 3x$	−3	(0, 5)
$y = 7x + 0.5$	7	(0, 0.5)
$6x + y + 8 = 0$	−6	(0, −8)

[10]

[1 mark for each correctly completed cell]

3. a) (0, 3) and (5, 0) **[1]**

b) (0, 2.5) and (10, 0) **[1]**

c) (0, −2) and (3, 0) **[1]**

d) (0, −8) and (10, 0) **[1]**

e) (0, −7) and (1, 0) **[1]**

f) (0, 3) and (−5, 0) **[1]**

g) (0, 2) and (−4, 0) **[1]**

4.

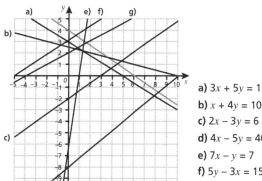

a) $3x + 5y = 15$

b) $x + 4y = 10$

c) $2x - 3y = 6$

d) $4x - 5y = 40$

e) $7x - y = 7$

f) $5y - 3x = 15$

g) $6y - 3x = 12$

[1 mark for each correct line]

5. a) $x = 1$ **[1]**

b) $x = -1.5$ **[1]**

c) $x = -1$ **[1]**

d) $x = 1.25$ [accept 1.2 or 1.3] **[1]**

e) $x = -1.75$ [accept −1.8 or −1.7] **[1]**

1. a)

x	−2	−1	0	1	2
x^2	4	1	0	1	4
$y = x^2 + 3$	7	4	3	4	7

[3]

[1 mark for each correct column]

b)

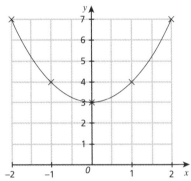

[3]

[2 marks for four points plotted correctly;
1 mark for at least three points plotted correctly]

2. a) $x = 1$ and $y = 2$ [1]

b) $x = -1$ and $y = -2$ [1]

c) $x = 0$ and $y = 1$ [1]

d) $x = -2$ and $y = 3$ [1]

e) $x = -3$ and $y = -2$ [1]

3. a)

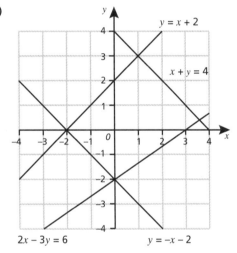

$2x - 3y = 6$ $y = -x - 2$

[4]

[1 mark for each correct line]

b) i) $x = 0$ and $y = -2$ [1]

ii) $x = -2$ and $y = 0$ [1]

iii) $x = 1$ and $y = 3$ [1]

4. a)

x	−3	−2	−1	0	1	2	3
x^2	9	4	1	0	1	4	9
$+ 2x$	−6	−4	−2	0	2	4	6
$y = x^2 + 2x$	3	0	−1	0	3	8	15

[3]

[1 mark for each correct row]

b)

x	−3	−2	−1	0	1	2	3
x^2	9	4	1	0	1	4	9
$- 2x$	6	4	2	0	−2	−4	−6
$y = x^2 - 2x$	15	8	3	0	−1	0	3

[3]

[1 mark for each correct row]

c)

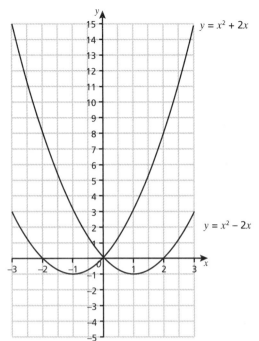

[2]

[1 mark for each correct line]

1. a) $x = 2$ and $x = -2$ [1]

b) $x = 2.4$ and $x = -2.4$ [accept 2.5 and −2.5] [1]

c) $x = 2.6$ and $x = -2.6$ [accept 2.7 and −2.7] [1]

d) $x = 1.7$ and $x = -1.7$ [accept 1.8 and −1.8] [1]

2. a) $x = 2$ and $x = 4$ [1]

b) $x = 1.3$ and $x = 4.7$ [accept 1.2 and 4.8] [1]

c) $x = 0.2$ and $x = 5.8$ [accept 0.1 and 5.9] [1]

d) $x = 0.6$ and $x = 5.4$ [accept 0.5 and 5.5] [1]

3. a) Area is $x(x + 4)$, so $A = x^2 + 4x$ [1]

b)

x	0	1	2	3
A	0	5	12	21

[2]

[1 mark for two correct values of A]

c)

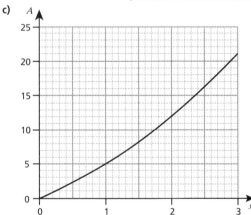

[1]

d) $A = 16.25\,m^2$ [accept 16 or 17] [1]

e) $x = 1.5\,m$ [accept 1.4] [1]

Pages 65–68: Compound Measures

1. a) 36 miles [1]
    b) 6 miles [1]
2. a) 6.5 s [1]
    b) 16.67 s [1]
3. a) 25 mph [1]
    b) 20 mph [1]
    c) 12.5 mph [1]
    d) 10 mph [1]
4. a) 6 g/cm³ [1]
    b) 6 g/cm³ [1]
    c) 4 g/cm³ [1]
    d) 4 g/cm³ [1]
5. a) 15 g [1]
    b) 22.5 g [1]
    c) 11.25 g [1]
6. a) 2 cm³ [1]
    b) 5 cm³ [1]

1. a)

Mass (grams)	Volume (cm³)	Category A, B or C
21	2	A [1]
18	3	C [1]
48.25	2.5	B [1]
19.3	10.5	C [1]

    b) There might be other metals with same density as silver and gold. [1]
2. a) 68 ÷ 2 = 34 litres/minute [1]
    b) 34 ÷ 2 = 17 litres [1]
        17 × £1.90 = £32.30 [1]
        Assumption: same rate of flow [1]
3. 100 grams is £2.40 ÷ 100 = 2.4 p per gram [1]
    250 grams is £6.19 ÷ 250 = 2.476 p per gram
    100 grams is better value [1]
4. 500 grams costs £0.85 ÷ 5 = £0.17 per 100 grams [1]
    400 grams costs £0.72 ÷ 4 = £0.18 per 100 grams
    500 grams is better value [1]

1. 550 g pack costs 400p ÷ 550 = 0.73 p per gram
    350 g pack costs 380p ÷ 350 = 1.09 p per gram
    180 g pack costs 150p ÷ 180 = 0.83 p per gram [2]
    [1 mark for two matching scalings, e.g. per gram, per 100 grams]
    Order is: 550 g pack, 180 g pack, 350 g pack [1]
2. a) 1 km = 1000 m or 1 h = 60 × 60 or 3600 seconds [1]
        5 m/s = 5 ÷ 1000 × 3600 = 18 km/h [1]
    b) Using a scale factor of 2.5, e.g.
        12.5 m/s = 2.5 × 5 m/s = 2.5 × 18 km/h
        or 12.5 ÷ 1000 × 3600 [1]
        = 45 km/h [1]
3. a) Sofia earns 30 × £15.36 or £460.80 [1]
        Manuel is paid £460.80 ÷ 36 = £12.80 per hour [1]

    b) 6 × £15.36 [1]
        = £92.16 [1]
4. a) Volume of block = 12 × 3 × 2 = 72 cm³ [1]
        Mass of block = 72 × 19.3 = 1389.6 g [1]
        Value of block = 1389.6 × £52 = £72 259.20 [1]
    b) 1389.6 ÷ 3 = 463.2 so 463 rings made [1]
        463 × £250 = £115 750 [1]
        Profit = £115 750 − £72 259.20 = £43 490.80 [1]

Pages 69–74: Right-angled Triangles

1. a) 0.5 [1]
    b) 1 [1]
    c) 0.7660 (4 d.p.) [1]
    d) 0.9903 (4 d.p.) [1]
2.

> You need to learn these trigonometric ratios. You can use SOHCAHTOA or another method to help you.

    a) $\cos \theta = \frac{adj}{hyp}$ [1]
    b) $\sin \theta = \frac{opp}{hyp}$ [1]
    c) $\tan \theta = \frac{opp}{adj}$ [1]
3. a) $\cos 50° = \frac{x}{5}$ [1]
        $5 × \cos 50° = x$ [1]
        x = **3.2** cm (1 d.p.) [1]
    b) $\tan 70° = \frac{y}{4}$ [1]
        $4 × \tan 70° = y$ [1]
        y = 10.989… [1]
        = **11.0** cm (1 d.p.) [1]
    c)

> Look at the diagram. Which side lengths do you know? Which ratio uses these side lengths? For example, here you know opp and hyp. $\sin = \frac{opp}{hyp}$

        $\sin 40° = \frac{w}{10}$ [1]
        $10 \sin 40° = w$ [1]
        w = **6.4** cm (1 d.p.) [1]
4. a) $\sin \theta = \frac{4}{5}$ [1]
    b) $\tan \theta = \frac{4}{3}$ [1]
    c) $\cos \theta = \frac{3}{5}$ [1]
5.

> Follow the steps in question 3.

    a) $\tan 25° = \frac{t}{6}$ [1]
        $6 × \tan 25° = t$ [1]
        t = 2.8 cm (1 d.p.) [1]
    b) $\sin 45° = \frac{u}{9}$ [1]
        $9 × \sin 45° = u$ [1]
        u = 6.4 cm (1 d.p.) [1]
    c) $\cos 60° = \frac{v}{8}$ [1]
        $8 × \cos 60° = v$ [1]
        v = 4.0 cm (1 d.p.) [1]
    d) $\tan 50° = \frac{w}{12}$ [1]
        $12 × \tan 50° = w$ [1]
        w = 14.3 cm (1 d.p.) [1]

1. a) $\sin m = 0.842$
   $m = \sin^{-1}(0.842) = 57.4°$ (1 d.p.) [1]
   b) $n = \tan^{-1}(2.4) = 67.4°$ (1 d.p.) [1]
   c) $p = \cos^{-1}(\frac{\sqrt{3}}{2}) = 30°$ [1]
   d) $q = \sin^{-1}(\frac{1}{\sqrt{2}}) = 45°$ [1]

2. a) $\tan \theta = \frac{5}{9}$ [1]
   $\theta = \tan^{-1}(\frac{5}{9})$ [1]
   $\theta = \mathbf{29.1°}$ (1 d.p.) [1]
   b) $\cos \theta = \frac{4}{7}$ [1]
   $\theta = \cos^{-1}(\frac{4}{7})$ [1]
   $\theta = \mathbf{55.2°}$ (1 d.p.) [1]
   c) $\sin \theta = \frac{3}{9}$ [1]
   $\theta = \sin^{-1}(\frac{3}{9})$ [1]
   $\theta = \mathbf{19.5°}$ (1 d.p.) [1]

3. a) $\sin x = \frac{11}{15}$ [1]
   $x = \sin^{-1}(\frac{11}{15})$ [1]
   $= 47.2°$ (1 d.p.) [1]
   b) $\tan y = \frac{5}{14}$ [1]
   $y = \tan^{-1}(\frac{5}{14})$ [1]
   $= 19.7°$ (1 d.p.) [1]
   c) $\cos z = \frac{9}{20}$ [1]
   $z = \cos^{-1}(\frac{9}{20})$ [1]
   $= 63.3°$ (1 d.p.) [1]
   d) $\sin a = \frac{5.4}{7.6}$ [1]
   $a = \sin^{-1}(\frac{5.4}{7.6})$ [1]
   $= 45.3°$ (1 d.p.) [1]

4. $\cos \theta = \frac{2}{2.3}$ [1]
   $\theta = \cos^{-1}(\frac{2}{2.3})$ [1]
   $\theta = 29.6°$ (1 d.p.) [1]

5. $\tan \theta = \frac{13}{24}$ [1]
   $\theta = \tan^{-1}(\frac{13}{24})$ [1]
   $\theta = 28.4°$ (1 d.p.) [1]

1. a) $\tan 35° = \frac{2}{p}$ [1]
   $p \times \tan 35° = 2$ [1]
   $p = \frac{2}{\tan 35°} = \mathbf{2.86}$ m (2 d.p.) [1]
   b) $\cos 42° = \frac{6.5}{q}$ [1]
   $q \times \cos 42° = 6.5$ [1]
   $q = \frac{6.5}{\cos 42°} = \mathbf{8.75}$ m (2 d.p.) [1]
   c) $\sin 30° = \frac{3.8}{r}$ [1]
   $r \times \sin 30° = 3.8$ [1]
   $r = \frac{3.8}{\sin 30°} = \mathbf{7.60}$ m (2 d.p.) [1]

2. a) CAD is a right-angled triangle. Labelling angle CAD as θ:
   $\sin \theta = \frac{3}{7.5}$ [1]
   $\theta = \sin^{-1}(\frac{3}{7.5})$ [1]
   $= 23.6°$ (1 d.p.) [1]
   b) BAD = 23.6° [1]

   Properties of isosceles triangle BAD = CAD

   c) As angle BAD = angle CAD, the line AD bisects (cuts in half) the angle CAB. [1]

3. a) $\tan 65° = \frac{h}{3.5}$ [1]
   $3.5 \tan 65° = h$ [1]
   $h = 7.505...$
   $h = 7.51$ cm (2 d.p.) [1]
   b) Area of triangle $= \frac{1}{2}bh$
   $A = \frac{1}{2} \times 3.5 \times 7.505...$ [1]
   $A = 13.135... = 13.14$ cm² (2 d.p.) [1]

4. Using Pythagoras' Theorem to find BD (hypotenuse of triangle CBD):
   $3^2 + 4^2 = BD^2$ [1]
   $25 = BD^2$, so BD = 5 cm [1]
   In triangle ABD: $\tan 40° = \frac{x}{5}$ [1]
   $5 \tan 40° = x$ [1]
   $x = 4.2$ cm (1 d.p.) [1]

   When the question doesn't tell you how to round your answer, round to a suitable degree of accuracy. In the question, all lengths are whole numbers, so a suitable degree of accuracy is to 1 d.p.

5. a) Label the length of the ladder x.
   $\cos 75° = \frac{1.1}{x}$ [1]
   $x \times \cos 75° = 1.1$ [1]
   $x = \frac{1.1}{\cos 75°} = 4.25$ m (2 d.p.) [1]
   b)

   $\cos \theta = \frac{3.5}{4.25}$ [1]
   $\theta = \cos^{-1}(\frac{3.5}{4.25})$ [1]
   $\theta = 34.6°$ (1 d.p.)
   $= 35°$ (nearest degree) [1]

6. a) Length OP = the radius of the circle = 1 unit [1]
   b) $\sin 80° = \frac{PQ}{1}$ [1]
   $\sin 80° = PQ$
   $PQ = 0.98$ units (2 d.p.) [1]
   c) $\cos 15° = \frac{OQ}{1}$ [1]
   $\cos 15° = OQ$
   $OQ = 0.97$ units (2 d.p.) [1]
   d) $\sin \theta = \frac{0.5}{1} = 0.5$ [1]
   $\theta = \sin^{-1}(0.5) = 30°$ [1]
   e) $\cos \theta = \frac{0.5}{1} = 0.5$ [1]
   $\theta = \cos^{-1}(0.5) = 60°$ [1]